MORE>
Distinct

MORE>
Distinct
Reclaiming holiness for the world today.

Calvin T. Samuel

INTER-VARSITY PRESS
36 Causton Street, London SW1P 4ST, England
Email: ivp@ivpbooks.com
Website: www.ivpbooks.com

First published 2018

British Library Cataloguing-in-Publication Data
A catalogue record for this book is available from the British Library.

ISBN: 978–1–78359–708–6
eBook ISBN: 978–1–78359–709–3

Set in Bembo 10.5/15 pt
Typeset in Great Britain by CRB Associates, Potterhanworth, Lincolnshire
Printed in Great Britain by Jellyfish Print Solutions

Contents

MORE>
Distinct

When Jesus came to the place, he looked up and said to him, 'Zacchaeus, hurry and come down; for I must stay at your house today.'

(Luke 19:5)

Chapter one

DISTINCTLY PROBLEMATIC

HOLINESS IS A 'MUFASA' WORD

In one of my favourite scenes in *The Lion King*, two hyenas are talking about the king of the jungle, Mufasa. For one of the hyenas, every time the name Mufasa is mentioned it sends a shiver down her spine. For many people, the word 'holiness' has the same effect; it has become something of a 'Mufasa' word.

You see, holiness has an image problem. In many quarters, it's a word which elicits negative connotations and legalistic impressions, too often conjuring ideas of 'holier than thou' and judgmental attitudes. Talk of holiness can easily make us feel inadequate, a measure of how far we've fallen short, a reminder of how much further we have to go.

Some years ago, I was asked to lead a church weekend event on this very theme. A number of people came up to me and said, 'I've been dreading this weekend for months!' FYI, that's never something the person leading your church weekend wants to hear. But it wasn't me they were dreading (at least that's what they said). They were dreading three days of hearing how badly they had failed in the pursuit of holiness.

There's something wrong with that picture, isn't there? If the gospel is good news, offering freedom, how is it that reflecting on holiness leaves some of us feeling trapped in a sense of inadequacy and failure? Why does this 'Mufasa' word send a shiver down the spine? Something is wrong; and I believe it is that for many, we so easily and so often misunderstand what holiness is, what it is for, and how it is expressed.

WHAT IS HOLINESS?

The best description of holiness that I've discovered comes from a fabulous woman called Ruth Etchells. Dr Etchells was a former principal of St John's College, Durham University, and the only woman to have held this role in the college's 100-year history. Indeed, she was the first layperson and the first woman to be appointed principal of an Anglican theological college, and this at a time fifteen years before the Church of England would ordain women as priests. She describes holiness in this way: 'Holiness is actually the shining dazzle of profoundest divine love exchanged continually within the Trinity and poured out for creation in all its forms for our deepest and most joyful good.'[1]

Three things strike me here. First, that holiness is a shining dazzle. Too few people are inclined to think of holiness as *shiny*. Most of us think of holiness as dour, hard work, sober and serious. Etchells reminds us that holiness is *attractive*. Second, that holiness is rooted in divine *love*. This not only reminds us that holiness and love are necessarily linked, but also that holiness is the core of God's being. If holiness is rooted in divine love, and God is Love, then whenever we talk about holiness, we are in fact trying to describe that which is the very heart of God. Third, holiness is rooted in divine *action*. Holiness is divine love poured out on creation. Who does the pouring out? God. Why is the love poured out? For our deepest and most joyful good. Holiness is rooted in the gracious action of God.

I grew up in a church that was very keen on holiness. It was emphasized, pursued, preached, taught and modelled; but it was not *gracious*. Instead it was judgmental and legalistic. I don't remember what I was taught about holiness, but I do know what I learned: holiness is a long list of rules and things that you don't do. In reality, this couldn't be further from the truth. You will never become holy because you work hard at it and keep all the rules. Throughout this book we will learn that holiness or sanctification is not so much about what we do or don't do; it's in fact about what God does and has already done in Jesus Christ. Holiness is the product of God's grace. You are saved by grace; you are also sanctified by grace. We are holy when we reflect something of God's goodness and glory in the world; holiness is not so much about sinless perfection as it is about Christlike reflection.

Moreover, holiness is for our deepest and most joyful good. I grew up viewing holiness like the spoonful of cod liver oil that my parents made me and my siblings take each day as a tonic for good health; it was good for us but tasted *vile*. But Dr Etchells' definition suggests that holiness is more like children's cough-and-cold syrup; it's both good for you *and* pleasant to the taste. Much like this sweet-tasting medicine, holiness will make us *well*; the path to human wholeness is by means of God's holiness.

HOLINESS IS TRANSFORMATIONAL

If holiness is not (as many of us have too often thought!) primarily about prohibited behaviour and rather about positive *action*, it follows that holiness is transformational. However, transformation is only truly valuable to the church if it is also *conformation* to the image of Christ and to the mission of God. Therefore, to pursue holiness is to acknowledge that all is not well. Individuals, communities and the world need to be both transformed and conformed to the image of Christ. In many ways, this is obvious. However, there are so many of us who do not really want to be transformed. We are who we are; we've spent a great deal of our time and energy figuring out who we are. In an age in which tolerance is the supreme virtue, the idea that anyone should tell someone else that he or she is in need of transformation feels a little uncomfortable. We may not mind a little spit and polish, but we don't really want to be transformed.

The truth is you need to be transformed; we need to be transformed; our churches, *good Lord*, need to be transformed. The problem with transformation is that challenges often have to be faced and sinfulness has to be acknowledged. To see the world by the light of the revelation and holiness of God is to have our vision corrected. It's like a visit to the optician: when we are finally offered the right lens the world suddenly becomes clear. That is the primary positive action of holiness; it transforms.

HOLINESS IS MISSIONAL

Holiness is not only transformational; it is also inherently missional. The two are closely linked. If holiness is divine love poured out on creation, then holiness becomes a powerful witness to the love of God and the power of the gospel to transform communities; holiness and love are integrally linked.

We see this in Jesus' reaching out to tax collectors and sinners, in the early saints martyred for their faith, in the early Methodists reaching out to the least and lowest; we see it today in Street Pastors, working in the unsociable hours when most of us are safely tucked up in bed. Christian communities that pursue holiness, as integrally linked with love, will inevitably end up in mission. Quite often they may not think that's what they're doing.

They are simply trying more fully to love God and to conform to the image of Christ. But we underestimate how powerful a community is that is shaped deeply and passionately by the love of God.

If some earlier Christians had had their way there'd be no sex, gambling, alcohol or sports on a Sunday. That vision of the world was rejected. Instead, when we understand holiness as positive action, as a reflection of Christ, it is deeply and powerfully attractive. I am not suggesting that holiness will not require that some forms of behaviour are prohibited. I am suggesting that the transforming power of God will address those far more effectively than judgmental humans or a list of dos and don'ts.

HOLINESS IS RADICAL

Where holiness is transformational and missional, it can also be radical – a far cry from the idea of stringency and prohibitions. Radical holiness is rooted in an optimism of grace; it is to believe that there are no limits on how much God's goodness and glory may be reflected. It is a way of seeing the world and all within it as pregnant with the possibilities of grace despite its brokenness, sinfulness and dysfunction.

We see this in the way Jesus engages with a hated chief tax collector, Zacchaeus, recorded in the Gospel of Luke. Tax collectors were generally seen as thieves, collecting not only tax but also their expenses (Luke 3:12–13). The taxes were paid to the Roman oppressors, with Jewish tax collectors exploiting Jewish people on behalf of Romans. Moreover, Zacchaeus was a *chief* tax collector. Needless to say, he was not well liked by the Jews.

As Jesus walks through town, Zacchaeus merely intends to look upon him from a safe distance, wanting to catch a glimpse of the miracle worker from Nazareth. Jesus has other ideas. He comes to where Zacchaeus is, calling him from hiding. There is urgency in his summons: *Hurry! I must stay at your house! Today!*

In that moment of inclusiveness, Jesus embodies a radical holiness which believes that there are no no-go areas in which God's goodness and glory may not be reflected. However, the action of divine grace is also evident in Zacchaeus' desire. What prompts a wealthy man, a person of some significance, to run and climb a tree just to catch a glimpse of Jesus? Men of a certain age and status did not often run in that time and culture. There was something drawing Zacchaeus to Jesus, something that he might not have been able to articulate, or even acknowledge, but prompting desire and action nonetheless. This is 'prevenient grace', the grace that goes before, the grace that draws us to God. In Jesus we see a radical holiness, willing to see God's grace reflected in the most tarnished and hated of tax collectors. And in Zacchaeus we see prevenient grace, drawing him towards such holiness.

A FRESH LOOK

Far from a view of holiness as rules and regulations that I – and I imagine many of you from time to time – have too readily adopted, this understanding of holiness begins to unpack the 'Mufasa' word and see it as reflecting the very nature of God: transformational, missional, radical and inherently linked with love. Throughout this book I am going to ask you to suspend your pre-held views on the subject – good and bad – so that we can begin to explore, understand and experience holiness afresh. It's one of the reasons I didn't call this book *MORE Holiness*. Unpacking what the Bible says on the topic, we are going to question what holiness is, how we get it and why (if at all!) we should want to pursue it. But first, I have a confession to make.

My name is Calvin and I'm a theologian . . .

WRESTLING WITH THEOLOGY

'Theology' is another of those 'Mufasa' words, which for many will not only send a shiver down the spine but may make you want to put this book down. But wait! If you have come to this book with questions – which I imagine you have – you are *already* wrestling with theology. Whenever we struggle to express and to make sense of our understanding of God, we are undertaking the task of theology. Not dry, boring, irrelevant theology (and I would argue that anything that is dry, boring and irrelevant can't be good theology!) but theology that is wrestling with who God is and who the people of God should be in response. Most of the theology in this book is implicit. However, as we are setting out, it feels appropriate, and indeed important, to be explicit about the theological task we are undertaking.

WHAT IS THEOLOGY?

The English word 'theology' comes from two Greek words: *theos* and *logia*. *Theos* refers to God and *logia* to speaking or studying. Just as biology is the study of *bios* or life, archaeology the study of *archeos* or ancient things, and anthropology the study of *anthropos* or humanity, so theology is the study of *theos* or God.

Simple enough, right? But this analogy begins to break down almost immediately. First, God is not simply an object or system that humans can study. God can't be observed through a telescope or microscope, or interviewed for divine opinions. God is a person who chooses whether to reveal himself. Second, God is also beyond human comprehension, so even if we were able to observe God we wouldn't be able to understand God adequately. Third, even if we did understand God fully we would struggle to express that understanding, because our language is too limited to describe all that God is. It's possible to observe and understand a sunset or rainbow, but we can't adequately describe what we have seen. Our language is too limited. If a sunset is beyond our description, what chance have we of describing God?

Don't put the book down yet. As God is not simply a subject or system, theology is possible despite human limitation, because God has chosen to reveal God's self. Divine revelation is what enables us to speak of God, to study and learn of God, because God has revealed by his grace what our senses alone would never be able to observe. Divine revelation, through the word of God supremely revealed in Scripture, and the act of God supremely revealed in Jesus Christ, enables theology; revelation enables us to undertake the theology of holiness.

A key element to note about theology is that it is a corporate undertaking. The word *logia* refers to speaking. Speaking implies a conversation partner. So theology, the speaking of and study of God, requires conversation about God.

HOW DO WE DO THEOLOGY?

If you're asking this question, you're not alone. For Christians, this conversation has been ongoing for two thousand years as we have wrestled to make sense of God's revelation in Jesus and in Scripture. God invites humanity into relationship, so that out of that relationship a deeper understanding of God, ourselves and the world becomes possible. In other words, theology is a discourse about God that is a response to God's revelation supremely expressed in Jesus Christ. It is happening every time we try to make sense of our beliefs and practices – whether or not you decide to use the 'Mufasa' words.

MAKING SENSE OF METAPHOR

A key element of our making sense of our theology, and one we will use in our journey with holiness, is the use of metaphor. As human language is not adequate to the task of capturing the glory and goodness and holiness of God, we are forced to use the imagery of metaphor. Even metaphors are inevitably inadequate, but that is not to underestimate how powerful a theological device metaphor can be.

When we say, 'The LORD is my shepherd' (Psalm 23:1), that is a powerful and striking metaphor. However, when we say that 'God is the king of all the earth' (Psalm 47:7), that is also a metaphor, for God is no more a king than a shepherd. Both terms are inadequate to describe who God is and who he is to us, but that is not to say that they are not hugely powerful images for aiding and expressing our understanding of God.

Perhaps one of the best-known visual metaphors in the UK is the London Tube map. We all know that the underground train tunnels aren't to scale; they don't extend in straight lines and are not painted in the colours that appear on the map. And yet, despite its limitations, the map is still an essential tool for any who want to navigate their way around London.

Over the course of this book we will engage with a number of models and metaphors for holiness. They won't always be labelled as such, in much the same way as the limitations of the Tube map aren't defined in small print somewhere. But that is what they are.

AN UNEXPECTED JOURNEY?

Fans of the film *The Hobbit* might remember that it was subtitled *The Unexpected Journey*. The hobbit's journey was both literal and metaphorical. By taking that journey he found out a great deal about good and evil and truth. He also found out about himself.

This book is an invitation to take a theological and historical journey through Scripture in the hope that, like the hobbit, we will discover a great deal about good and evil, truth and ourselves. Beginning in the Old Testament and journeying to the New will allow us to undertake a thorough and serious exploration of Scripture to see how ideas of holiness were built over time. It will also allow us to trace where our (often misplaced!) conceptions of holiness come from and better locate our contemporary understanding of holiness.

Many complex issues need to be rooted in their history if they are to be deeply understood. We'll never understand #BlackLivesMatter unless we take the time to revisit the American Civil Rights struggles of the 1950s and 1960s. Understanding why feminist perspectives are so important requires that we revisit our history to remember that not so long ago women were considered inferior to men. Similarly, a biblical understanding of holiness requires a journey back to our roots in the earliest parts of Scripture. Before we set off, perhaps we should consider one central question that remains: *why* is holiness important? It is to that question that we are going to turn first.

You shall be holy,
for I the LORD
your God am holy.

(Leviticus 19:2)

Chapter two

DISTINCTLY PRECIOUS

THE COMPLEXITY OF HOLINESS

Holiness is a complex issue. As Christians we know that we ought to be holy and yet we know we are sinful. We disagree on what holiness looks like and how it is attained, and how far we can truly become holy. We know that to pursue holiness is our responsibility and yet we know that we cannot become holy unless the Holy One makes us holy.

Into our fog come the words of Leviticus 19:2: 'You shall be holy, for I the LORD your God am holy.' In exploring the idea of 'the holy', we need to explore three questions. First, why is holiness important? Second, how is holiness attained? Third, what does holiness look like?

WHY IS HOLINESS IMPORTANT?

The concern with holiness is something that we find throughout the pages of the Bible. In the Old Testament, we see this concern expressed in the sacrificial system and purification laws, for example the food rules in Leviticus 11 and purity rules in Leviticus 12 – 16. Later in Leviticus we find not only the command to be holy but also all sorts of laws to enable people to be holy in the presence of God and within community. For example, the pursuit of justice in Leviticus is understood to be an outworking of the holiness of God's people.

Similarly, among the Old Testament prophets, especially Elijah, Isaiah, Amos and Ezekiel, we find a consistent call to holiness which requires justice. The book of Job is very much concerned with the question of holiness, both Job's holiness and God's. The Psalms begin by contrasting the way of the wicked with the way of the righteous, and conclude with praise in the sanctuary of the Holy One.

In the New Testament, the concern with holiness continues. We find it in the ministry of Jesus in the Gospels, for example in Jesus' Sermon on the Mount, not least the declaration in Matthew 5:48 that we should be perfect as our heavenly Father is perfect. Similarly, in the epistles, whether of Paul in Thessalonians and Romans, or of Peter, or of the anonymous writer to the Hebrews, we find a repeated and consistent call to holiness.

It seems pretty clear that Scripture is very much concerned with the question of holiness. Nonetheless, the question remains: why is it important? Put simply, holiness is important because it's important to God; not because it is God's hobby but because it is at the heart of who God is. Hear the words of Leviticus 19:2 again: 'You shall be holy, for I the LORD your God am holy.' When God says 'I am holy' it is not like me saying 'I am tall, dark and handsome'; because while this may be true, it is only one facet of me as a person! No, when God says 'I am holy' it is much closer to what I mean when I say 'I am Calvin'. I am not merely telling you *a fact about me*, what I am called; rather I am trying to tell you *who I am*.

Holiness, similarly, is not merely one of God's characteristics; rather it *is who God is*. Holiness is the quintessential nature of God. Old Testament scholar Walter Moberly argues that 'holy' is tantamount to a definition of the nature of YHWH.[1] John Hartley states it more stridently: 'Holiness is not one attribute of Yahweh's among others; rather it is the quintessential nature of Yahweh as God . . . Holiness thus distinguishes Yahweh from all other creatures.'[2] Hartley continues, 'In the entire universe . . . [YHWH] alone is intrinsically holy.'[3] This, I suggest, is the primary reason why holiness is important, for when we seek after holiness we seek far more than to be lovely people; we seek far more than to be committed to justice; we seek far more than to be people of integrity. Rather, much more importantly, when we seek after holiness, we seek nothing less than to become like God.

HOW IS HOLINESS ATTAINED?

The answer to this question is a paradox. On the one hand, holiness is beyond our reach. If holiness is intrinsically who God is, humans cannot be holy unless God makes us holy. In Exodus 3, we see Moses meeting with God at the burning bush, where God declares: 'Remove the sandals from your feet, for the place on which you are standing is holy ground' (v. 5). I suspect that the ground was not holy because it had said the sinner's prayer, confessed its faith in Jesus Christ, and sought after a second definite work of grace, a second blessing of holiness. Rather, the ground was holy simply because God was present and God's holiness infected, as it were, the very ground. Something rubbed off. Similarly, as humans we need something to rub off from God on to us if we are to have any hope of being holy. Holiness is a work of grace. God has to do it or else it is not grace.

And yet, holiness is not merely a passive pursuit. Note what Leviticus declares: 'You shall be holy.' It is a command, a directive. We are instructed to be holy. This indicates that holiness is not only about God's gracious gift; it is also about human pursuit. This is the paradox of holiness. We cannot become holy unless God shares God's holiness with us; and yet we never become holy apart from seeking it, working at it and pursuing the Holy One.

Leviticus does not merely instruct Israel to be holy; it also gives clear indications of what this might involve. Interestingly, little of what follows in Leviticus 19 is ritualistic stuff. Certainly, there are instructions about sacrifices to be offered, but most of it refers to how we should love our neighbours as ourselves, especially those who are poor and powerless. Moreover, we find that much of Leviticus 19 is a restatement of the Ten Commandments of Exodus 20:

1 Have no other gods (vv. 4, 31)
2 Do not worship idols (v. 4)
3 Do not profane God's name (v. 12)
4 Keep the Sabbath (vv. 3, 30)
5 Honour your parents (vv. 3, 32)
6 Do not murder (implied in vv. 17–18)
7 Do not commit adultery (vv. 20–21)
8 Do not steal (vv. 11, 13)
9 Do not lie (v. 11)
10 Do not covet (implied in vv. 20–25)

It is also in Leviticus 19 that we find the raw material for Jesus' declaration that we should love our neighbours as ourselves (v. 18). Indeed, I believe that Jesus must have been a great reader of Leviticus. When Jesus taught in Matthew 5 that it is not enough not to commit murder but we are also not to hate, that was not an original idea; we find it here in Leviticus 19:17. When Jesus tells the story of the Good Samaritan in Luke 10, that too is not an original idea; we find instructions to love the alien in Leviticus 19:34.

Leviticus is not satisfied with merely instructing the people of God to be holy; it also gives clear indications of expected behaviour in everyday life. Holiness in Leviticus is not an abstract, theoretical, doctrinal concept. It is a lived experience of the grace of God. It is a paradox: on the one hand a gift gracefully bestowed and on the other hand something never attained without obedience to God's word.

WHAT DOES HOLINESS LOOK LIKE?

Into this paradox comes the question: what does holiness look like? Unless we have some idea of what holiness looks like, how will we recognize it when we see it? How will we know whether we have attained it? The answer to this question is both simple and complex.

If it's true that holiness is the very core of who God is, then the answer to the question is mind-numbingly simple. What does holiness look like? It looks like God. To be holy is to be godly, to value what God values, to speak as God would speak, to reflect God's very being. Again, we see a great example of this in Exodus where we find Moses being in the presence of God on Mount Sinai. Having spent so much time with God, Moses descends from his mountaintop experience with his face so irradiated with the glory of God that he has to wear a veil. Similarly, holiness is to reflect God's person and glory.

But this is where it moves from mind-numbing simplicity to mind-aching complexity, for who knows what God looks like? You may have heard the story of a child busily at work drawing a picture. Her mum asked her what she was drawing. She replied, 'I'm drawing a picture of God.' Her mum said, 'Really? But nobody knows what God looks like.' The child replied, 'They will when I'm finished!'

What does God look like? We don't know for sure; and yet we are not left clueless. God sent Jesus to give us some clues as to who God is and what holiness looks like. To be holy is to be like Christ, for he is the ultimate example of human holiness. Jesus taught many things, but perhaps most importantly he taught by his actions, not least his actions on the cross.

What Jesus demonstrates, then, is that to be holy is to love our neighbours as ourselves; it is to love the Lord with all our heart, soul, strength and mind; it is to give ourselves completely over to God even if it leads to suffering and death. What does holiness look like? Holiness looks like God; holiness looks like Christ.

Moreover, if holiness looks like God and God is invisible, then holiness also is invisible. If you come from the same strand of holiness tradition that I come from, that idea is problematic because, as I discovered, there are many in that tradition who want holiness to be visible. So they become very legalistic to demonstrate this. Ultimately, however, like God, holiness is invisible. Nonetheless, although God is invisible we can see evidence of God's presence.

Similarly, holiness, although invisible, is evident by continuing transformation through grace; sanctification is growth in grace and holiness. Holiness becomes visible through continuing transformation by God's grace.

This idea of growth in holiness implies that we are growing towards an end; that holiness is possible here and now, and yet it is also the ultimate end of relationship with God, not fully consummated until the end of the age. Here, we touch on the inherently eschatological – 'now and not yet' – nature of holiness. John puts it this way: 'what we will be has not yet been revealed. What we do know is this: when he is revealed, we will be like him' (1 John 3:2).

So, what we have in human experience of holiness, then, is a foretaste of the heavenly banquet, a deposit of what is to come, the first fruits of the harvest of the end of the age. This perhaps helps to explain the now-and-not-yet nature of holiness. First fruits are indeed real fruit but not the whole of the harvest. A deposit is hard cash in hand but only a fraction of the due sum. So it is with human experience of holiness through the Spirit; holiness is of this age but primarily of the age to come. To pursue holiness is thus to seek to experience the age to come breaking into our present age.

A PRECIOUS PARADOX

Leviticus 19:2 is a call to holiness for *all* who are the people of God. Because holiness is the heart of who God is, holiness must be the heart of who we are as God's people. If holiness is the heart of God's very being, we must resist the temptation to reduce the human pursuit of holiness to a simplistic super-spirituality. Holiness is complex; it is costly, often requiring working out in pain. It is entirely dependent on God – people, spaces, objects or times that are described as holy can only be so because they in some way relate or belong to the Holy One. At the same time, holiness is never attained without effort: seeking, hungering and thirsting for righteousness on our part. Thus, holiness remains a mystery.

Often, we do not recognize ourselves to be holy but others are able to see evidence of God's grace in us. When Moses' face was aglow with the glory of God, he could not see it but everybody else could (Exodus 34:29–35). One reason for this is that the more we grow in grace and holiness, the more we become aware of our sinfulness and of our ongoing need for sanctification, for God's holy ones are not incapable of sin – holy people can and do sin. I suspect therefore that the more holy we become, the less holy we feel.

So we return to those words of Leviticus: 'You shall be holy, for I the LORD your God am holy.' How far is this true of your experience of your Christian community? How far is this your individual experience? Let's make that journey together. Let's dare to ask God to sanctify us by the power of the Spirit so that we might truly be holy as God is holy.

And they were calling to one another: 'Holy, holy, holy is the LORD Almighty; the whole earth is full of his glory.'

(Isaiah 6:3 NIV)

Chapter three

DISTINCTLY DIVINE

HOLINESS IS A DIVINE ATTRIBUTE

The vision of Isaiah in chapter 6 is one of my favourite passages in Scripture. I preach and teach from it repeatedly. It's a story of how the prophet Isaiah receives a divine call to ministry. More than that, it offers an insight into the awesome holiness of God.

One of the most striking things about that vision is the seraphim calling to one another and saying repeatedly: 'Holy, holy, holy is the LORD Almighty; the whole earth is full of his glory.' As I mentioned briefly in the previous chapter, Walter Moberly, a leading Old Testament scholar, describes this passage, with its threefold repetition of 'holy, holy, holy', as tantamount to a definition of the nature of God.[1]

If you've ever struggled to understand or to express what you understand about holiness, you are not alone. Most people I know struggle to express what they understand holiness to be. Actually, that's not true. Most people I know rarely talk about holiness at all and those who do often use well-known definitions such as 'holiness is to be set apart' without giving too much further thought as to what that means or why that should be the case. We are rarely on comfortable ground when we talk about holiness. Isaiah's vision perhaps gives us good reason for this, because when we talk about holiness we are trying to wrestle with the very nature of a God upon whom seraphim do not even dare to look! Jacob Milgrom, a world-renowned scholar on Leviticus, offers this elegant description of holiness:

> Holiness is assigned to God alone. Holiness is his quintessential nature ... distinguishing him from all other beings. If certain things are termed holy – such as land (Canaan), person (priest), place (sanctuary), or time (festival day), they are so by virtue of divine dispensation.[2]

Holiness, then, becomes a mark of the presence of the divine, or an indication of the presence of God's essential characteristic. It's striking that the seraphim of Isaiah 6:3 have little else to say about God beyond 'holy, holy, holy'. If it is true that holiness is essentially who God is, then we do not have language sufficient to the task of describing what we mean by holiness.

HOLINESS IS WHO GOD IS

If holiness is who God is, God's quintessential nature and the core of God's very being, how could finite humans ever presume to know what is the core of God's infinite being? Obviously, we cannot – unless God has chosen to reveal to us that which we could never figure out for ourselves. Our theology of holiness, that is to say, our understanding of holiness, is based on this very idea of divine self-revelation.

If it is true that holiness is distinctly divine, for it is who God is, how does this shape our understanding of holiness? Several elements emerge. First, it means that holiness is not humanly possible. To tell people to be holy, if by 'holy' we mean who God is, is to demand of them more than they can give. Recognizing that holiness is not humanly possible is critical, especially for all who long to be holy. It explains why we fail. However, as Jesus reminds us in Matthew 19:26, 'For mortals it is impossible, but for God all things are possible.' We can't make ourselves holy, but thankfully we know a God who can.

Second, holiness is not primarily about what we do; it's more about who and whose we are. Again, I'm not suggesting that holiness has no relevance for our behaviour. Rather, I'm saying that our behaviour is not the route to achieving holiness. Every time you have felt guilty for choosing football over church, every time you have felt smug because you have ticked your 'read

Bible today' check box, every time you have fervently prayed for holiness, you have become in no way more or less holy. Holiness cannot be achieved through our behaviour. If holiness is who God is, then it is similarly our identity and belonging which enable us to be holy, rather than what we do. Our behaviour stems from who and whose we are.

Third, holiness is thus not primarily an ethical category but rather a relational one. Again, I do not mean to suggest that holiness has little to do with ethics. Far from it. Indeed, Jesus declared *twice* in Matthew 7: 'You will know them by their fruits' (vv. 16, 20). So, our ethics are a matter of priority for a holy people. Because of who we are, and whose we are, our ethics matter, not only to us but ultimately to God. Nonetheless, to say that holiness is divine is also to say that we can only be holy if the Holy One makes us so. So, when we describe a person, a place or thing as holy, we are in fact saying that that person or place or thing is in some way in relationship to the God who alone can make holy. We can't speak about the holy without reference to and *relation* to the Holy One.

HOLINESS AS APPLIED THEOLOGY

Fourth, holiness is not primarily an individual category but a communal one. This is where instructions in the Old Testament for God's people to be holy as God is holy become particularly interesting. Put another way, such instructions ask a very pointed question: given the nature of God's holiness, what does this imply for God's people? This pointed question was addressed to the whole community and not just its religious leaders, whether priests, Levites or Nazirites.[3] Therefore, to put it bluntly, the whole community, including its worst sinners, was viewed as capable of attaining the requisite holiness. How is this possible? How is a whole community, including its worst sinners, capable of being holy as God is holy? Because of who and whose we are as people of God. Our community can be holy *because* God is holy, and *we belong* to God.

Whenever someone was introduced to my grandfather, a man deeply shaped by ancient Antiguan cultural mores, his first question was always 'Who are your people?' His basic assumption was: if I can identify your people, if I know which family clan you belong to, if I know which village you are from, only then do I really know who you are. As one who grew up in Antigua in that strongly tribal family culture, I was a little surprised to discover when I arrived in the UK in my mid-twenties that I was expected to have had a crisis of some kind as I tried to respond to the existential question 'Who am I?'

I had no idea this was a question I was supposed to have figured out, because it hadn't crossed my mind. I suspect I never felt the need to ask the question 'Who am I?' because I always knew the answer to the question 'Whose am I?' I am a Samuel. My family and clan identity were never in doubt. Even to this day, I think of myself first as a member of that family (I am a Samuel) and only secondarily as an individual within that family (I'm Calvin). My family identity is stronger than my individual identity, and indeed shapes that individual identity. Our identity as the people of God must be stronger than and help to shape our individual identity and behaviour.

Scripture does not only instruct the people of God to be holy; it also gives specific examples of what this means for them. For example, passages such as Leviticus 19, Exodus 22 and Deuteronomy 24, which describe what God's holy community should be like, are not primarily concerned about sacrifices, Sabbaths and the sanctuary but rather are concerned about the poor, the disabled, love for neighbours, care for the alien and stranger, integrity and justice.[4]

So, what does holiness look like in community? It looks like farmers leaving some of the harvest for the poor, employers not exploiting their workers, and the able-bodied not taking advantage of the deaf and blind; it looks like loving your neighbours as yourself, and standing against injustice wherever you encounter it (see Leviticus 19:9–13; Deuteronomy 24:20–22; Exodus 22:21–31).

Holiness is distinctly divine. It is best understood as God's quintessence; holiness is who God is. This understanding of holiness underpins all the additional nuances of holiness that we will go on to explore together in later chapters, and should be understood as the master metaphor which unlocks all the others.

'Therefore come out from them, and be separate from them, says the Lord, and touch nothing unclean; then I will welcome you, and I will be your father, and you shall be my sons and daughters, says the Lord Almighty.' Since we have these promises, beloved, let us cleanse ourselves from every defilement of body and of spirit, making holiness perfect in the fear of God.

(2 Corinthians 6:17 – 7:1)

Chapter four

DISTINCTLY COMPLEX

HOLINESS IS MORE THAN SET APART

Since the earliest times described in the Bible, people of God have been wrestling with the idea of holiness. What does it mean to be holy and what models and metaphors might we use to understand it? Perhaps the most common way of thinking about holiness is as being set apart; that is, set apart for God's special purposes. Indeed, there are hints of this in the title of this book, *MORE Distinct*.

I grew up in a church that is part of the holiness movement. One of the texts that I heard again and again as I was growing up was 2 Corinthians 6:17 – 7:1 in which we hear an explicit connection between separation from the unclean thing, being welcomed by God, and the perfecting of holiness. Paul in this passage is, of course, quoting the Old Testament, most probably Isaiah 52:11. But the idea of separation from the unclean as a requirement for holiness goes back even further, to the first five books of the Bible, the Pentateuch, especially Leviticus.

It will not have escaped your notice how often the book of Leviticus has been referenced thus far in the early parts of this book. Now might be the time to address the elephant in the room. Leviticus is hardly likely to be most people's favourite book of the Bible. For most of us, Leviticus is that eccentric great-aunt who we try to avoid admitting is related to us. Oh, and by the way, Auntie Leviticus has something similar to Tourette's syndrome, so you never know what outrageous thing she's going to say next!

To the uninitiated, Leviticus seems arcane and just possibly *insane*. This is a book that lists how many days a woman is unclean after she gives birth to a girl as opposed to the number of days if she gives birth to a boy (Leviticus 12:1–5)! If you've ever heard that there are bits of the Bible that forbid the wearing of clothes made from different materials (so you'd better repent if you're reading this wearing a cotton–rayon mix), that'll be eccentric Auntie Leviticus (19:19). However, Auntie Leviticus is more than she seems. Get to know her well and you'll discover that she is certainly eccentric, often arcane, but certainly not insane. She has really valuable things to say that need to be said.

Therefore, our focus on Leviticus is intentional, and important not least because, as Jacob Milgrom, one of the world's leading scholars on Leviticus, argues, the theme of the entire book of Leviticus is holiness.[1] Not only is Leviticus important because of its emphasis on holiness; it's also important because it underpins much of the discussion of holiness in other parts of the Bible that we explore in later chapters, as we shall see.

So how is holiness understood in the Pentateuch, especially in the book of Leviticus? Philip Jenson, a biblical scholar with a research interest in holiness, insightfully argues that holiness in the Pentateuch is distinctly complex. He argues that holiness is envisaged using at least five differing models or metaphors.[2]

Holiness is viewed in terms of

1 separation – being set apart;
2 power – for example a consuming fire, burning bush, dangerous cloud;
3 the wholly 'other' – holiness exceeds everything worldly;
4 God's realm or sphere – holiness refers to anything or anyone that belongs to God's realm or sphere of existence;
5 divine character or quintessence – holiness is the core of God's very being.

We have already considered the fifth point, the idea that holiness is divine. Taking the other four – holiness as set apart, power, the wholly 'other', and God's realm or sphere (the latter two points are similar and so considered together) – let's reflect on these models and metaphors of holiness in turn, in the hope that (like the visual metaphor of the London Tube map) they help us better navigate some of the earliest biblical understandings of holiness.

HOLINESS AS SET APART

Even a cursory reading of the Old Testament indicates that ideas of being set apart and holiness are closely intertwined. Holiness as being set apart or separate is a significant theme in Leviticus, hence the food rules and purity regulations. The anthropologist Mary Douglas helpfully suggests that Old Testament rules of avoidance might best be understood as holiness given physical expression. Thus, dietary laws and regulations about sacrifices were meant to be signs which at every turn inspired meditation on the oneness, purity and completeness of God.[3]

It is less clear from these biblical texts *why* holiness should require separation. Could it be something to do with the idea of belonging to a transcendent God? Or is separation required because of the fragility of holiness? Holiness can seem fragile; impurity entering a holy sphere may profane the holy; and what was once holy may apparently lose its holiness until ritually cleansed (see Leviticus 21:12; Numbers 19:20).

In this 'set apart' model, holiness feels a bit like keeping post-surgery patients away from people who have colds or other infections. Alternatively, being set apart might have more to do with protection *from* the consuming power of holiness. Holiness is so affective and so powerful that the holy must be handled carefully. So, which is it?

HOLINESS AS ENERGY OR DESTRUCTIVE POWER

As a theological student I was privileged to be taught by a wonderful, godly and holy man called Gordon Thomas. He taught me to see that in Leviticus the separation required by holiness probably has more to do with its potentially destructive power than its fragility. In Thomas's view, the story of the exodus is in large part a story of a God who desired to live among his people, but for their safety there was needed a *cordon sanitaire* between the holy and dangerous God and the sinful people he chose to dwell among.[4]

God himself graciously provided this place of safety in the form of the sanctuary or the Tent of Meeting (Exodus 40). For those unfamiliar with it, the Tent of Meeting was the place where the ark of the covenant of the Lord was kept and where Moses, the leader of the people of God, would meet with God to receive instructions during the time of the exodus. The ark of the covenant was an expression of something of the concentrated presence of God, a presence which was also symbolized by a pillar of fire by night and a pillar of cloud by day. Whenever Moses met with God in the Tent of Meeting, the pillar of cloud would descend to the entrance of the tent (Exodus 33:9–10).

This concentrated divinity was dangerous for anyone who was not holy. If you've seen the film *Raiders of the Lost Ark* you'll have some idea of how destructive the concentrated divinity represented by the ark of the covenant could be to the unworthy people who opened it. If you haven't seen the film, as soon as you've finished this section, put the book down and go find it online or order it. It'll be worth the interruption!

The Tent of Meeting, the tabernacle, was in later centuries superseded by the temple, and the ark of the covenant was placed in the holy of holies, at the point of the temple furthest from the entrance. Only the high priest could enter this holy space, and only once per year. This was the ultimate depiction of holiness as set apart. Here was a means of separating a dangerously holy God from a dangerously sinful people. The regulations outlined in the Israelite sacrificial cult enabled sinful people to live with the Holy One in their midst without fear of being consumed by the potentially destructive power of God's holiness.

Perhaps one of the most striking biblical stories outlining the potentially destructive power of the holy is to be found in the account of Uzzah in 2 Samuel 6. The story concerns the moving of the ark of the covenant from the house of Abinadab, where it had lodged for twenty years, to the city of Jerusalem, King David's newly established capital city. The ark was transported on a new cart drawn by a team of oxen, and driven by Uzzah and Ahio, the sons of Abinadab. As the cart reached the threshing floor of Nacon,

Uzzah reached out his hand to steady the ark because the oxen had caused it to shake. In the act of touching the ark, Uzzah was struck dead. King David was so distraught and terrified by this that he abandoned his attempt to relocate the ark and instead left it in the house of Obed-edom for three months. During that time Obed-edom's household was extraordinarily blessed because of the presence of the ark. As Lucy discovers in C. S. Lewis's The Chronicles of Narnia, Aslan is not a tame lion, nor even a safe one . . . but he is good.

HOLINESS AS CONTAGION

Related to the idea of holiness as power is the idea of holiness as contagion, whereby contact with the holy renders objects or places holy. Put simply, holiness is *affective*. John Hartley, a Leviticus scholar, explains:

> God's holiness is contagious. Wherever his presence is, that place becomes holy . . . Because only Yahweh is intrinsically holy, any person or thing is holy only as it stands in relation to him. Thus, there are degrees of holiness depending on the proximity of an item or person to Yahweh.[5]

The way we think about holiness is often shaped by the way we think about sinfulness. *Sin as act* is often portrayed in legal terms: the breaking of a law. However, *sin as being* – in other words, why we are so inclined to commit sinful acts, our propensity towards *sinfulness* – has been visualized primarily in three ways: as enslavement, as stain and as sickness.

Sinfulness as enslavement is perhaps best captured in Romans 7: the things that I do not want to do, those are the things that I do. I explore the idea of enslavement a little further in chapter 8 so I won't say any more here.

For an example of the idea of sin as stain or impurity, consider the words of the great prayer of confession that is Psalm 51:

> Have mercy on me, O God,
>   according to your steadfast love;
> according to your abundant mercy
>   blot out my transgressions.
> Wash me thoroughly from my iniquity,
>   and cleanse me from my sin . . .
> Create in me a clean heart, O God,
>   and put a new and right spirit within me.
> (vv. 1–2, 10)

A similar sentiment may be observed in many popular hymns, such as the lines:

> What can wash away my sin?
> Nothing but the blood of Jesus.[6]

Indeed, I remember as a child in the Caribbean singing, entirely without irony, the following hymn:

> Whiter than the snow,
> Whiter than the snow,
> Wash me in the blood of the Lamb,
> And I shall be whiter than snow![7]

Only when some visiting American missionaries found this hugely amusing did it occur to me that as a little black boy who had never seen snow in his life, it might be a little odd to sing a prayer to be made whiter than snow! The language of washing, blotting out, purifying and cleansing as a response to human sinfulness uses the imagery of a stain or impurity on the human soul to describe sinfulness.

For an example of the idea of sickness, consider the words of Jesus in Mark 2:17: 'Those who are well have no need of a physician, but those who are sick; I have come to call not the righteous but sinners.' That sentiment is explicit in the old African-American spiritual:

> There is a balm in Gilead
> To make the wounded whole,
> There is a balm in Gilead
> To heal the sin-sick soul.[8]

Perhaps much better known is the classic description of sinfulness as blindness:

> Amazing grace (how sweet the sound)
> That saved a wretch like me!
> I once was lost, but now am found,
> Was blind, but now I see.[9]

The language of healing, wounding, physicians and blindness as a response to human sinfulness uses the imagery of sickness to describe sinfulness.

The images of sickness or stain are so powerful that it is easy to forget that they are metaphors; they can lead us to imagine sin as a virus or substance when in fact sin is primarily a relational term. The idea of sin only makes sense when there is a deity to be offended. It is that relationship to the deity which causes something to be perceived not merely as wrong but also as sinful. Sin is, therefore, a meaningless concept in an atheistic framework. It's one reason why 'sin' is such an uncomfortable word in contemporary culture.

If you've ever tried to share your faith with your non-Christian friends you will know that it's quite often the idea that we are sinners which causes people to run into difficulty. 'What sins?' your friends may ask. 'How can we be sinners if we're good people?'

And sin is such an old-fashioned word too. The term 'sin taxes' is used to describe the taxes levied on alcohol, tobacco, gambling, or other objects and habits of widespread disapproval seen as vaguely immoral.[10]

The opposite of sinfulness is holiness, also a relational term. It's primarily in this way that holiness is affective or contagious. If God alone is holy, then only those who in some way are touched or marked by God can be holy. Only those who *relate* to the Holy One can be holy.

HOLINESS AS OTHERNESS OR GOD'S SPHERE

Holiness as power has some overlap with the idea of holiness as God's sphere. In the words of the biblical scholar Philip Jenson: 'If the "holy" is defined as that which belongs to the sphere of God's being or activity, then this might correspond to a claim of ownership, a statement of close association, or proximity.'[11] For example, it may be argued that the Sabbath is holy because God rested on that day and has declared ownership of the Sabbath (Exodus 20:8–11). The Sabbath, then, reminds us of God's claim to ownership not only of the Sabbath but also of all time.

Old Testament scholar Christopher Wright helpfully reminds us that while the idea of 'sphere of being' is a difficult concept for us to grasp, it is key to understanding the Old Testament perceptions of the Israelites in terms of their relationship to God.[12] Holiness as being under God's sphere is certainly key to understanding the idea of the Israelites as a holy people: they were holy precisely because they belonged to God and not because they were morally or ethically holy, or distinctive in any other way. However, it is not merely an imitation of God that is in view here; the motivation for this imitation is also rooted in God's action. It is because God has chosen the people of Israel and brought them into his sphere, because he has brought them out of slavery and into the Promised Land, that they are to be holy.

CORPORATE HOLINESS

This idea of the people of God being holy by virtue of their belonging to the divine sphere brings to the fore the issue of corporate holiness. Put simply, the fact that the Israelites constituted the holy people of God did not presuppose that every member of the community was individually holy. In fact, much of the discussion of holiness as power earlier in this chapter is predicated upon the difficulties of having a dangerously holy God living among dangerously sinful people, and yet it is these dangerously sinful people who were described as God's holy people. Holy people who are dangerously sinful? If this is not to be a contradiction in terms it requires thinking of holiness in a way that allows for the existence of the sinful.

It seems clear to me that when Scripture speaks of Israel as God's holy people, that holiness is conceived primarily in corporate terms. In fact, the sacrificial system with its various means of atonement presupposes individuals who fail to be what they are, the holy people of God. If we return to the Sabbath, its designation as a holy day is not based upon an assumption that each of its 24 hours or 1,440 minutes is holy; it is rather to do with the day as a whole being chosen by God as his day of rest. In a similar way, the people are a holy people not because they constitute a collection of holy individuals, but only because they belong to God's sphere, rooted in the fact that he has called and chosen them. Nonetheless, that is not to say that there is no relationship between this corporate holiness and both corporate and individual character and conduct. Despite the fact that their holiness is not based upon their lack of individual sinfulness or, indeed, possession of individual holiness, God's people are, nonetheless, required to behave in ways that reflect the divine.

SET APART FROM AND TO

Separation, or being set apart, is very much part and parcel of the biblical presentation of holiness. Holiness requires both *separation from* that which is profane or sinful and *separation to* that which is holy and divine. In parts, this separation seems to imply that holiness can be fragile and needs protection from the impure. In other parts, this separation seems to be for the protection of the impure. Leviticus 15:31 seems to capture both nuances: 'Thus you shall keep the people of Israel separate from their uncleanness, so that they do not die in their uncleanness by defiling my tabernacle that is in their midst.' But holiness is more than separation. It is also an attempt to describe the power of God and God's sphere of influence. To describe something or someone as holy is at the very least to describe them not merely as a set-apart one, but also as something or someone marked and transformed by the power of God and under God's sphere of influence. Holiness is distinctly complex. And it is all the more wonderful for that fact.

For the LORD your God
is God of gods and
Lord of lords, the
great God, mighty
and awesome, who
is not partial and takes
no bribe, who executes
justice for the orphan
and the widow, and
who loves the strangers,
providing them with
food and clothing.

(Deuteronomy 10:17–18)

Chapter five

DISTINCTLY INCLUSIVE

HOLINESS AS SOCIAL BIAS

One of the striking things about the God of the Old Testament is God's intolerance of idolatry. You get a hint of this in the Ten Commandments: 'You shall have no other gods before me', and 'You shall not make any idols, for I am a jealous God'. But why is God so concerned about idolatry if there *is* only one god?

Devout Jews, throughout history and up to the present time, are required to recite each day the Shema: 'Hear, O Israel: The LORD is our God, the LORD alone. You shall love the LORD your God with all your heart, and with all your soul, and with all your might' (Deuteronomy 6:4–5). Let me assure you that this concern about idolatry is not for God's benefit. It's not that God has an inferiority complex which requires his ego to be boosted regularly. No, it is rather because idolatry often has quite a nasty sting in the tail. It allows idolaters to ignore the fact that the Holy One of Israel is a God of justice. Ours is a God of justice because he is a holy God.

Jesus puts his finger on this when asked: what is the greatest commandment? Like a good Jew he responds by quoting the Shema: 'You shall love the Lord your God with all your heart, and with all your soul, and with all your mind. This is the greatest and first commandment.' However, he goes on to say, 'And a second is like it: "You shall love your neighbour as yourself." On these two commandments hang all the law and the prophets' (Matthew 22:37–40).

God is intolerant of idolatry because idols only require us to honour them with sacrifices or gifts. However, our God is a God of justice; in order to serve *this* God we must also be committed to justice. Through the prophet Amos, God puts it starkly: 'Take away from me the noise of your songs; I will not listen to the melody of your harps. But let justice roll down like waters, and righteousness like an ever-flowing stream' (Amos 5:23–24).

One of the particular ways in which God's commitment to justice can be observed is in God's concern for the powerless. Those who have power will almost always get justice, eventually: 'We'll see to it and we won't rest until justice is served.' For those without power, justice is too often an ideal that they've heard about but not often experienced.

LEARNING FROM DEUTERONOMY

In the Old Testament, the powerless are often described using four repeated tropes: the widow, the orphan, the alien, the poor. One of the reasons they are powerless is because in that time and culture only adult male Israelites had access to and protection under systems of justice. So those who were widows, orphans and aliens had no representatives in the justice system to stand up for their interests. Hence, God is repeatedly depicted as being concerned for and on the side of the powerless. If you have an electronic Bible look up the words 'widow' and 'orphan' and see how often they come up. Go ahead, do it now. I'll wait . . .

In the culture of the day, concern for widows and orphans was very common across a wide range of Ancient Near Eastern (ANE) people groups. What was novel in Israel was concern for the alien and stranger. They too were to be cared for. Greek Old Testament scholar Myrto Theocharous's work on sexual trafficking is very helpful here. She discusses the following passage:

> Slaves who have escaped to you from their owners shall not be given back to them. They shall reside with you, in your midst, in any place they choose in any one of your towns, wherever they please; you shall not oppress them.
> (Deuteronomy 23:15–16)

Theocharous argues persuasively that Deuteronomy 23:15–16 is unique in the ancient world:

> While ANE law dictates that the right thing to do is to return a runaway slave to his or her master or country, biblical law breaks away from this norm and forbids such a 'deportation.' Giving asylum to such refugees was a distinctive of Israelite law marking them apart from all other nations.[1]

Often these terms – widows, orphans, aliens – were largely interchangeable, not because widows are the same as aliens, but because they describe people on the edges of society: those who have no access to its justice systems and who often fall through the cracks in its support structures.

My grandfather was the eldest son of a widow. His father died in 1917 when he was nine years old. The death of the breadwinner in Antigua's patriarchal culture of the day, and at a time when the whole world was at war, meant that my grandfather and his family moved from having a fairly comfortable lifestyle, by the standards of that period, to becoming homeless within the space of a few months. And they remained homeless for five years. Imagine how much worse his situation would have been if he had lost both parents as an orphan.

The God of justice is concerned for the powerless because all too often they do not have a just or fair share of the world's resources or access to its systems of justice; often the system works against them rather than for them. By way of example, young women and girls who are coerced into prostitution in the more developed nations of the world can find themselves arrested and then deported to their original countries, charged with illegal immigration and prostitution rather than being rescued from illegal detention and modern-day slavery.[2]

Deuteronomy chapter 10 describes the giving of the Ten Commandments. This was God's second attempt. On the first attempt, while Moses was fasting on Mount Sinai for forty days and nights and receiving the tablets of stone on which were inscribed the Ten Commandments, the Israelites were busy building a golden calf, one of their earliest experiments with idolatry (see Deuteronomy 9:8–21). In Deuteronomy 10:12–13, the commandments are summarized:

> So now, O Israel, what does the LORD your God require of you? Only to fear the LORD your God, to walk in all his ways, to love him, to serve the LORD your God with all your heart and with all your soul, and to keep the commandments of the LORD your God . . .

However, verses 17–19 makes it absolutely clear who is this God whom the Israelites are to serve:

> For the LORD your God is God of gods and Lord of lords, the great God, mighty and awesome, who is not partial and takes no bribe, who executes justice for the orphan and the widow, and who loves the strangers, providing them with food and clothing. You shall also love the stranger, for you were strangers in the land of Egypt.

That sentiment is expressed rather more forcefully in a set of instructions in Deuteronomy 24:17–22:

> You shall not deprive a resident alien or an orphan of justice; you shall not take a widow's garment in pledge. Remember that you were a slave in Egypt and the LORD your God redeemed you from there; therefore, I command you to do this . . .

The God whom we serve is a God of justice, not because he is committed to a set of high-minded principles but rather because that is who God is. The God we serve is a God of justice; God is love and that love requires justice. When we describe a 'God of justice' we need to be clear what our model of justice is. Most of us with a Western upbringing and outlook think of justice using law court imagery. We might imagine justice as being blind and therefore impartial. Everyone is treated the same. Justice ensures that the law is upheld so that transgressors are punished and the innocent are protected. The English word 'justice' is derived from the Latin word *iustitia* and comes with Latin legal nuances preloaded. The problem with this concept of justice is that by the time you get to the law court, something has already gone wrong. It is a rectifying kind of justice.

However, the model we should be looking at is a communal or family model, where it is not the law that is the primary image but the relationships of the community. Here justice is no more blind than parents are blind to the varying needs of their children. The ideal is not for everyone to receive the same, but for everyone to receive what he or she needs, because we don't all need the same things. Justice in this model is about fairness and right relationship. 'Righteousness' is the word that might more naturally describe this model of justice.

The concept of righteousness is captured in the Hebrew word *tzedek* which is itself translated in the New Testament by the Greek word *dikaiosune* (pronounced *di-kayo-soon-ay*). If you struggle to pronounce it, think *yippee-ki-yay* from the *Die Hard* films. Then again, maybe that's not such a good idea. Scratch that. From *dikaiosune* we get the English word 'justification', as in justification by faith. But this is a word which, like *tzedek*, primarily describes right relationship. To be righteous is not primarily to perform right actions, though righteousness requires this. Rather, it is primarily to maintain right relationship, which often requires performing right actions. This is not a rectifying kind of justice to address things that have gone wrong, but a foundational kind of justice, seeking to establish things in the way they really ought always to have been.

Clearly both models are part of our picture of God. However, it is a relational foundational model that is paramount rather than a legal rectifying model. The law court can punish wrongdoers and establish the rights of the otherwise unrepresented, such as widows, orphans and aliens; but it can't reconcile communities.

To assert that God is a God of justice is also to make a statement about our doctrine of creation. We believe that God has good intentions for this world, that we have been created to have life to the full. Human flourishing is part of God's divine plan for us. Jesus declared: 'I have come that they may have life, and have it to the full' (John 10:10 NIV). Given this conviction, part of God's approach to human flourishing is to seek to embed and to embody divine justice, or righteousness, within our communities. Scripture is clear that the people of God are expected to join with God in his mission of justice. To love God, we must also love our neighbour and all creation, and demonstrate this in how we live and act. It's noteworthy how Deuteronomy chapter 24 repeatedly reminds the Israelites that they had once been slaves in Egypt, that they too had once been aliens and poor, widows and orphans. This is a reminder of human solidarity. The reality is that there is no *them*; there is only *us*.

LEARNING FROM THE PROPHETS

The Deuteronomic concern for the widow and orphan, alien and poor, gets picked up in later prophetic tradition. Biblical prophets are not so much concerned with telling the future as they are with pointing people back to what they know already.

Just as Leviticus stands out in the priestly tradition for what it tells us about holiness, so does Isaiah among the prophets. Not only is the book of Isaiah among the most significant of the prophetic writings, but it also stands out because it makes most use of the language and concepts of holiness. The word 'holy' (*qâdôsh* in Hebrew) appears more frequently in Isaiah than in any other prophetic book.

Old Testament scholar Christopher Wright helpfully identifies two aspects of the ministry of biblical prophets. First, their *theological basis*, whereby God is the presupposition for all they say, and, second, their *social bias*, whereby the prophets are uniformly on the side of the poor, weak, oppressed and dispossessed.[3] We see this in prophetic books such as Amos and Isaiah, and also in the words of earlier prophets who left us no books; for example, in Elijah's denunciation of King Ahab because of his murder of Naboth (1 Kings 21). Under these two headings of 'theological basis' and 'social bias', then, let's further explore holiness in prophetic thinking.

THEOLOGICAL BASIS

'The Holy One of Israel' is perhaps the most significant way in which God is described in the book of Isaiah. Many biblical scholars believe that the book of Isaiah was compiled by three different authors: proto-, deutero- and trito-Isaiah. But interestingly, the phrase 'the Holy One of Israel' occurs throughout the early, middle and latter parts of the book. We find a similar designation also in Jeremiah. YHWH is above all the Holy One of Israel.

This is not unimportant. The holiness to which the people of Israel are called, and the standards of the Holy One to which they are pointed by the prophets, is not a novel development but part of their identity and heritage as the people of God. The holiness of God is taken as a given by the prophets, and the things of God are, therefore, naturally holy.

Isaiah's vision

There are some things that we see which change our lives for ever. For some, it's the first sight of their newborn child. For others, it's a world-changing event: the toppling of the Berlin Wall or the falling of the Twin Towers. For yet others, it's a flash of spiritual insight. The prophet Isaiah falls into this latter category. He had a vision of the Lord seated in holiness and majesty, and it's a vision that continues to inspire people to this day.

In Isaiah's vision, six-winged seraphim are the primary actors on the stage. All at once they fly, cover their faces and feet, and call to one another with voices so huge that the threshold of the temple shakes. And they cry repeatedly, 'Holy, holy, holy is the LORD of hosts; the whole earth is full of his glory [or: the fullness of the earth is his glory]' (Isaiah 6:3).

Some scholars suggest that these seraphim are not to be seen as angels. They are perhaps better understood as effigies of foreign gods.[4] If so, this is a vision of a God so great and holy that even those idols – which other nations worship as gods – themselves offer continual worship to this God of gods. Despite this, the primary object of Isaiah's vision is not seraphim but God's very self, as he is in his holiness.

Since the prophets take the holiness of God as a given, the things of God are, thus, naturally holy. Whether it be his holy mountain, holy arm or holy temple, the prophets took for granted that the things of God are holy. This was also to be the case with his people; they were to be holy as he is holy.

SOCIAL BIAS

If human holiness is derived from God's character, then the nature of human holiness is necessarily informed by the nature of God. Unsurprisingly, human holiness as perceived by the prophets is closely linked with God's moral integrity. This is not to imply that moral integrity is synonymous with holiness. Holiness is much more complex than simply being equated with morality. Nonetheless, moral integrity can exemplify holiness.

Holiness in Israel was a summons to the people to aspire to the justice and compassion characteristic of their summoning God.[5] It is no coincidence that the role of the prophet comes to the fore during the time of the monarchy. The prophets tended to address themselves to the powerful on behalf of the powerless, urging them to reconnect justice and holiness. This is certainly the case with Nathan, whose story is recorded in 2 Samuel 12.

Nathan was prophet when King David seduced Bathsheba, got her pregnant and then had her husband murdered so that he could keep the scandal hidden. After a suitable time had elapsed, David then married the widowed Bathsheba, who was possibly unaware that her husband had been intentionally killed. When Deuteronomy instructs us to care for widows, I don't think this is what it had in mind!

At this point, David has got away with it. No one knows of his adultery and the steps he's taken to cover it up. It is precisely then that the prophet Nathan is sent by God to denounce David on behalf of Uriah the Hittite, whom he has killed, and Bathsheba, whom he has exploited. What no one else could have known, God revealed to the prophet. Prophets call for a model of holiness that is resolute in its demand that all have a place, even those on the margins. If Isaiah 6 exemplifies the theological basis of holiness, the 'highway of holiness' in chapter 35 typifies its social bias, for Isaiah's view of holiness is inextricably bound up with social justice.[6] It's distinctly inclusive.

Isaiah 35:8 describes a holy way, or highway of holiness, a unique expression in Scripture. The New Revised Standard Version translates it: 'A highway shall be there, and it shall be called the Holy Way; the unclean shall not travel on it, but it shall be for God's people; no traveller, not even fools, shall go astray.' It's commonly translated in a similar way in other Bible versions; the majority view is that this should be understood as a highway of holiness on which the unclean are not welcome.

However, eagle-eyed readers will note that this verse has a footnote in most modern translations pointing out that the phrase translated 'travel or pass along it' can also be translated 'pass it by'.[7] This changes the meaning of the verse entirely. Rather than excluding the unclean from travelling on the holy way, the alternative reading suggests that the unclean shall not pass it by; that is, they shall not fail to see it.[8] Old Testament scholar Walter Harrelson makes an argument for this particular understanding which I find compelling: that the reference to the unclean is not as an indication of their *exclusion* but rather of their *inclusion* in Isaiah's eschatological vision, alongside the blind, deaf, lame and dumb of verses 5–6.[9]

In my view, this makes much more sense of the idea of a holy highway. Given that many exiles would be unclean almost as a matter of course as a result of living outside the Holy Land without access to priests and the sacrificial system, there would be little point in envisaging a holy highway to bring exiles back home if those who are unclean can't use it!

On this reading, Isaiah 35 is a vision of the return of exiles along a holy highway to become part of a redeemed society, which is for all people, including those normally excluded or marginalized, such as the blind, deaf, lame and dumb, and the unclean.[10]

GOD OF JUSTICE

God is a God of justice because he is a holy God. Our worship of him must reflect that fact. So, any idol or empty worship which does not have a commitment to justice is never appreciated by God. Instead we demonstrate our love for God by ensuring that the poor and the powerless, the aliens and the strangers, the widows and the orphans are cared for. Those who are interested in holiness will care deeply about social justice. They care deeply about those on the margins. Holiness is distinctly inclusive.

The LORD said to Satan, 'Have you considered my servant Job? There is no one like him on the earth, a blameless and upright man who fears God and turns away from evil.'

(Job 1:8)

Chapter six

DISTINCTLY HUMAN

HOLINESS IS NECESSARILY RELATIONAL

Earlier in this book I argued that holiness is distinctly divine. In this section, I'm going to argue that holiness is distinctly *human*. How can these contradictory claims be held together?

In Christian understanding, humanity is created in the image of God and intended for relationship with him. Holiness is not humanly possible, but through divine grace 'what is impossible for mortals is possible for God' (Luke 18:27). Through grace, holiness becomes humanly possible.

Perhaps one of the best examples of human holiness in Scripture is to be found in the book of Job, which at first glance does not appear to be about holiness. For starters, the word itself does not appear in over forty chapters. But in fact, as we will see, holiness is the key question which underpins the whole story of Job; not merely whether Job is as holy as he appears, but also whether a God who initiates such undeserved suffering as Job endured can rightly be understood to be holy.

In case you're unfamiliar with the story of Job, let me bring you up to speed. The narrator introduces Job from the very first verse as one who was blameless and upright, a person who feared God and turned away from evil (Job 1:1). That seems to me to be a pretty good description of what holiness looks like from a human perspective. The next two verses describe Job's large family, and his great possessions – so valuable that he is considered the greatest of all the people of the east (Job 1:2–3). The following verses go on to indicate the exceptional level of his pietistic scrupulosity (that's honestly a thing!). Job routinely offers sacrifices for each of his children to sanctify them just in case they may have blasphemed God in their hearts. The narrator makes no explicit link between these two facts about Job, his exceptional holiness and exceptional wealth, but this is the critical question posed by the satan:[1]

> Does Job serve God for nothing? Have you not put a fence around him and his house and all that he has, on every side? You have blessed the work of his hands, and his possessions have increased in the land. But stretch out your hand now, and touch all that he has, and he will curse you to your face. (Job 1:9–11)

The accusation is very clear. Job appears very holy only because God has lavished generosity on him. Were God to become less generous, then Job's true commitments would show. This is the reason why all that Job has must be removed. It would be unsatisfactory to both reader and accuser for God merely to assert that Job does indeed fear God for nothing. Now that the question has been raised, it needs to be addressed head on. The entire premise of the book, then, is about the question of holiness. Is Job as holy as he appears?

What happens next is both terrible and terrifying. In short order, Job loses all his possessions, his children are killed in a storm, and he is ultimately struck down by a disease which results in him being covered from head to toe with loathsome sores. However, in all this Job did not sin (Job 1:22). He maintained his uprightness and blamelessness. Towards the end of chapter 2, Job is visited by three comforters who believe that such catastrophic misfortune must be divine punishment of some kind for his sinfulness. So, for much of the next thirty-nine chapters, Job argues for his innocence and argues with God for his apparent absence and silence. Chapters 3–41 are therefore filled with long speeches disputing the nature of God, justice and righteousness, before the narrative resumes in chapter 42. As a consequence, many people read the book of Job by reading the first two chapters and then skipping to the final chapter. That's a mistake. Some of the most interesting things in Job occur in these disputation speeches.

One of the most attractive things about the story of Job is its earthiness. Here is a man presented as reaching the epitome of human holiness, portrayed as exceptionally godly. Despite this wonderful description, life for Job is not a bed of roses. Instead we see him struggling to work out his holiness while he tries and fails to make sense of his bereavement and apparent abandonment by God.

In the story of Job, we encounter a man who spends much of the time angry with God, partly because of all that has happened to him, but mostly because he believes that what has happened to him is unjust. Despite what his friends believe, he knows that the terrible things that have happened to him are not the result of some hidden sin on his part.

It seems to me that this is part and parcel of what it means to say that holiness is distinctly human. It has to be worked out in the midst of a life that is, for most of us, far from ideal. Some characters in the Bible seem to have their act together; they are wonderful, faithful and exemplary people. Some Christians appear to be very much like those biblical characters; life is straightforward and they appear healthy and happy and holy and blessed. Things always seem to work out well for them.

For lots of us, however, this is not the case; we are more like Job. Not only do bad things happen to good people, but they have happened to *us*. It's one thing for God to be holy. But what does it mean and what does it look like to be holy when your world is falling apart and slipping through your fingers? That's what the book of Job offers us. A glimpse of holiness through the lens of pain, loss, bereavement and illness. There are three things in particular to notice about the story of Job, a book which I think is intended to be subversive from the start and to challenge easy stereotypes about holiness.

OUTSIDE THE LAND

First, the story of Job is set outside the land of Israel, in the land of Uz. Biblical scholars have not been able to locate any place called Uz but know it was not in Israel.[2] In his book *Contagious Holiness*, Old Testament scholar Craig Blomberg observes: 'Job may well not have been Jewish.'[3] This view is strengthened by the fact that for most of the book when Job speaks, he does not address God in the way most Israelites would. Rather than YHWH, the Israelite name for God, *el* or *elohim*, a generic word meaning 'god', is used instead.

That Job is outside the land implies he is outside the covenant. It is noteworthy that the book makes no reference to any of God's past 'saving acts'. When Israelites got into trouble, they could recall God's past dealings with the patriarchs and matriarchs of the nation: 'The God who was faithful to Abraham, Isaac and Jacob, and Sarah, Rebekah, Rachel and Leah, the God who was faithful to Moses, Joshua and Caleb, will also be faithful to us.' However, this was not a route open to Job. His relationship with God has no stated historical or covenantal basis. He therefore has no grounds on which to trust that the God who has acted in certain ways in the past will do so in the future. Job's faithfulness and holiness is thus based entirely on a simple but direct relationship with God. It is all the more remarkable for this fact.

That Job, a man from Uz, is singled out for being blameless and upright at the very least implies that holiness is not the sole preserve of God's covenant people. Indeed, one may go further and argue that the book implies that in order to find the best example of human holiness one is best off looking outside Israel. Holiness can be found in unexpected places among unexpected people.

OUTSIDE THE CULT

Second, Job is also outside the sacrificial cult. Once Job is afflicted by loathsome sores, which would have been viewed by Israelite readers as a form of leprosy, he would be unclean and therefore normally disqualified from participating in sacrifices or entering holy spaces such as the temple.[4] The fact that Job is found in the ash heap, scraping himself with a potsherd (Job 2:8), and visible though unrecognizable from a distance (Job 2:12), at the very least suggests that Job may be among the outcasts of society after his infection.[5] Despite this, towards the end of the book as God breaks his silence and finally speaks to Job, he concludes by vindicating

Job and rebuking Job's 'comforters'. God addresses Eliphaz, one of these men:[6]

> My wrath is kindled against you and against your two friends; for you have not spoken of me what is right, as my servant Job has. Now therefore take seven bulls and seven rams, and go to my servant Job, and offer up for yourselves a burnt-offering; and my servant Job shall pray for you, for I will accept his prayer not to deal with you according to your folly; for you have not spoken of me what is right, as my servant Job has done.
>
> (Job 42:7–8)

Job is presented here in the role of both priest and intercessor for his comforters and referred to by God as 'my servant Job' four times in quick succession, the very designation by which he was singled out by God for being exceptional at the beginning of the book (1:8; 2:3). Crucially, all of this precedes his restoration, which occurs at 42:10.

Regardless of whether it is leprous Job or his comforters who offer this sacrifice (the text is unclear), there is no suggestion that Job's standing with God, his holiness, is in any way affected by his illness and consequent uncleanness. While he is still covered in sores from head to toe, it is *his* prayers which God will hear and not theirs. In making this statement, the story of Job paints a radical picture of a holy leprous intercessor, perhaps even a holy leper-priest!

In addition to challenging our conceptions of holiness, this text invites reflection on human experiences: is sickness related to sinfulness? Does God care for both Israelite and non-Israelite alike? Can holiness be found outside the covenant people? All of these are in addition to the story's central question, which is not *why* do bad things happen to good people but *how* should good people respond when bad things happen?[7] Perhaps most significantly, the story of Job makes it clear that human holiness is possible through a relationship with God that holds true even in the most trying of circumstances.

OUTSIDE THE NORM

Third, the book of Job does not stop at its radical suggestion of a holy Gentile leper. Instead, the very idea of God's holiness is explored and we discover God portrayed in a way that is very much outside the norm in biblical texts. It is God who draws Job to the attention of the accuser (1:8; 2:3), God who gives permission to the accuser to cause Job's misery (1:12; 2:6), God who appears to need confirmation of the true reasons for Job's fidelity (1:9–11) and God who allows this misery to continue until finally bringing it to an end at 42:10.

In 1952, Carl Jung, one of the most significant figures in psychology, published his controversial book *Answer to Job*, in which he subjects the God of the story of Job to psychoanalysis. He observes: 'From the human point of view, Yahweh's behaviour is so revolting that one has to ask oneself whether there is not a deeper motive hidden behind it.'[8]

He goes on to note that God is ultimately responsible for the 'dark deeds' that follow in quick succession and adds: 'This is further exacerbated by the fact that Yahweh displays no compunction, remorse, or compassion . . . he flagrantly violates at least three of the commandments he himself gave out on Mount Sinai.'[9]

One of the really interesting things about the story of Job is that it does not attempt to defend God's actions towards Job. When God does finally answer, Job receives no explanation for why his life has fallen apart. Instead, God affirms his sovereignty and Job is challenged for his audacity in questioning his creator. Nonetheless, at the end of the story God affirms that what Job has said about God, much of which is harsh, is in fact right (Job 42:8).

The writers challenge the idea that holy people have a good life. Job doesn't, God offers him no explanation for this, and the authors feel no need to defend God in this matter. God's sovereignty is simply upheld. However, human responsibility is also upheld. Throughout the story Job holds on to his integrity and rejects the idea that since God is sovereign, God can do whatever God likes. Rather, Job challenges God to justify his actions. Job even goes as far as to express his hope in a kinsman redeemer, a vindicator, who might ensure that he shall see God in his flesh; that is, stand face to face with the respondent in his court case (19:25–27)![10]

MORE LESSONS FROM JOB

At least three significant insights into holiness may be gleaned from the experiential reflection in the story of Job. First, holiness for the authors of Job is internalized; one is not holy because of what is on the outside but because of what is on the inside. Second, as a result of this internalization, holiness cannot be contained or constrained. Even those outside the covenant can be holy, not least because God is bigger than any covenant and even those who are seen to be unclean can be holy. Third, holiness represents a tension between divine sovereignty and human responsibility. How do we know that Job is holy? Because God describes him as such on a number of occasions (1:8; 2:3). Job is holy because God declares him to be holy. This is the divine sovereignty pole of human holiness. At the same time, Job's holiness is preserved because of his efforts. He does not 'sin with his lips' (2:10) despite all that befalls him; he maintains his integrity and blamelessness (9:20–21). This is the human responsibility pole of human holiness. The authors of Job offer us a perspective into holiness which is couched, not in terms of victory over sin, but in terms of integrity and the fear of the Lord sustained even *in extremis*.

The Bible presents multiple images of a holy human. At one extreme is Moses whose face is set aglow by the glory of God (Exodus 34:29–35). Perhaps the other extreme is Job who doesn't look holy to his friends and who is angry with God because he feels unjustly treated. Job is holy because he's in deep relationship to God. That relationship means that Job's holiness not only reflects God, but also reflects who Job is. Job's relationship to God is so profound that, for him, worshipping God and arguing with God are not contradictions but emerge from the same place of deep relationship. I grew up in a family of five children. We argued all the time. We also teased one another mercilessly. We still do. Part of the reason that we argue and tease is because we love one another and trust one another. Profound love is expressed not only in sweet words but also in hard ones.

Job offers us a perspective on human holiness that is almost unique, and therefore all the more precious. Here is a vision of holiness that is distinctly human, rooted in the messiness of life, intertwined with pain and loss, illness and anger, weakness and conflict, but which is nonetheless marked by integrity and faithfulness to God. There is something earthy and true about this picture. This is holiness that is distinctly human.

A leper came to him begging him, and kneeling he said to him, 'If you choose, you can make me clean.' Moved with pity, Jesus stretched out his hand and touched him, and said to him, 'I do choose. Be made clean!'

(Mark 1:40–41)

Chapter seven

DISTINCTLY CHRISTOCENTRIC

HOLINESS AS OFFENCE RATHER THAN DEFENCE

One of the striking things about Jesus in the Gospels is the way in which he engaged with those who were ritually and morally impure. Jesus was to be found eating with tax collectors and sinners; he touched lepers and dead people; he consorted with demoniacs and bleeding women. This did not conform to the assumptions and conventions of Jesus' day, any more than it does to ours today.

As a result, Jesus soon found himself in conflict with the religious establishment. Some of the questions raised by those in authority are captured in the Gospels. Why does Jesus eat with tax collectors and sinners (Mark 2:16)? Why don't Jesus' disciples wash their hands before eating (Mark 7:5)? Other questions are not captured in the text, but a number of Jesus' actions almost certainly would have raised questions. Why did you touch the leper (Mark 1:40–41)? Do you not know that he will make you unclean? Why have you consorted with a demon-possessed man who lives in an unclean Gentile land, among tombs and in close proximity to two thousand pigs (Mark 5:1–13)? This is impurity upon impurity upon impurity!

Jesus was not simply being controversial. He certainly wasn't seeking merely to stand out. (Why do Christians, who are called to be holy, all too often settle for being weird?) However, I do believe that Jesus was living out his understanding of what it means to be holy, and that was in radical opposition to what the Pharisees understood holiness to be.

HOLINESS IN ISRAEL

With regard to the question of holiness, two of the most significant groups within Judaism during the time of Jesus were the Essenes and the Pharisees.[1] The Essenes understood holiness in terms of purity of life, requiring separation *from* society. John the Baptist, perhaps, is the best-known biblical character who fits this ideal.

The Pharisees, in contrast, understood holiness as purity of life requiring separation *within* society. For them, the pursuit of holiness implied full obedience to the demands of Torah. Crucially, they believed that for the presence of the holy to be possible within society, it was necessary for ordinary members of society to comply with rules of purity normally applied only to priests, and then only when they ministered in the temple.[2]

Biblical scholar Marcus Borg argues, insightfully, that Jesus and his followers offered an alternative view of what it meant to be holy *within* society and that it is this competing vision of holiness which accounts for the numerous conflicts between Jesus and the Pharisees.[3]

IS HOLINESS A BIT LIKE SEX?

There is a bit of a problem; the Gospels don't seem overly interested in the question of holiness. Indeed, Jesus offers very little *direct* teaching on the theme of holiness and sanctification, and the language of holiness is not prominent within any of the Gospels. One notable exception occurs in John 17, in Jesus' prayer that God would sanctify the disciples in truth. However, just because the vocabulary of holiness isn't explicit, it doesn't mean the idea isn't present. In this regard, holiness is a little bit like sex.

Brits employ a bewildering range of words to talk about sex. I make this point when I visit churches to talk about holiness, before asking my listeners to share the range of terms they employ to talk about sex (when we do talk about it; we *are* Brits after all!). Some of the more unusual include 'fellowship' (seriously?!) and 'tea' (homage to the popular sexual consent video);[4] but my all-time favourite is 'a bit of "How's your father?"' I have never understood how that phrase has come to mean what it means. Anyway, as with sex, so it is with holiness: the absence of the word does not indicate the absence of the thought.

So, where in the Gospels do we look to gain insight into Jesus' views on holiness if in fact we may be looking for different vocabulary? As Borg argues, Jesus offered an alternative view of what it meant to be holy *within* society. This competing vision accounts for the fact that the Gospels devote so much space both to detailing Jesus' conflicts with Pharisees, and to portraying him as repeatedly undertaking actions which indicate how his views conflict with theirs. Because of this, it follows that exploring some of these conflicts should offer insight into Jesus' understanding of holiness in the Gospels.[5]

WHY DID PURITY MATTER?

New Testament scholar Jimmy Dunn insists that if we are to grapple adequately with Jesus' understanding of holiness we must explore his attitude to purity and impurity.[6] Dunn draws on the work of Jacob Milgrom, who argues that of the two opposite pairs, holy/profane and pure/impure, the dynamic categories are holy and impure. The profane and the pure are simply the absence of their opposites, as darkness is not a quality in itself but simply the absence of light. This, he argues, makes impurity the effective antithesis to the positive power of holiness.[7]

If holiness is envisaged as a clean bleached garment that one must keep pure, then dirtiness or impurity can be a potential threat to that aim. In which case, impurity will be perceived as dynamic and potentially encroaching, while holiness will be perceived as static. In order to maintain holiness, the impure needs to be kept away from the holy for fear of besmirching it. By contrast, if we envisage holiness not as the bleached garment itself, but rather as the bleaching agent, then holiness is perceived as a dynamic, and contact with the impure does not have any effect on it; rather the impure is cleansed and made potentially holy. No one worries about the effect some impurity might have on their bleach! But we do worry about inadvertently getting bleach somewhere we did not intend. Holiness is seen as powerful and therefore potentially a little bit dangerous.

One's attitude towards impurity offers some insight into one's understanding of holiness. It is striking that the Pharisees were very concerned that holiness might be besmirched by impurity. That's why they were concerned about eating with tax collectors and sinners, and the washing of hands. It is equally striking that Jesus was entirely unconcerned about these things. Holiness was, for Jesus, a power which cleanses uncleanness and dissolves impurity rather than a status under constant threat from the unclean.[8]

These conflicting understandings of holiness, I suggest, lie at the heart of some of the conflicts between Jesus and the Pharisees. For

Pharisees, the holy needed to be protected from being soiled by the unholy and impure (hence all the rules!). Holiness in this view is defined almost by reference to what is *excluded*. This is an understanding of holiness rooted in status with God and expressed through faithfulness to Torah.

Jesus' understanding of holiness, equally rooted in faithfulness to Torah, seems to be as a dynamic power, with a missional imperative that the holy be put into close contact with the common, unclean, sinful or perhaps even profane with the consequence of transforming it. Jesus had an offensive understanding of his own holiness which conquered impurity.[9]

OFFENSIVE RATHER THAN DEFENSIVE HOLINESS

My suspicion is that many churches today have a view of holiness that is more rooted in a defensive posture than an offensive one. The church tradition I grew up in certainly did; holiness was the bleached garment and it was our job to keep it clean by keeping away from sin. But if we see holiness as the bleaching agent, that which makes the garment clean, then it is instead an offensive tool that has no other purpose than to clear impurity.

Viewed through this lens a number of Jesus' actions take on particular significance. When Jesus touches the leper (Mark 1:40–45) Jesus is not made unclean; rather it is the leper who is cleansed. Jesus then instructs the leper to follow the Levitical instructions for ritual purification following recovery from leprosy. Intriguingly, however, nowhere in Mark's Gospel is Jesus portrayed as undertaking ritual cleansing himself. According to Levitical law, Jesus should have been made unclean by touching a leper. However, rather than Jesus becoming defiled it is the leper who is cleansed.

This is not an isolated incident. Jesus follows this up with a number of other dubious actions in Mark's Gospel. He consorts with a Gentile demoniac (Mark 5:1–20), who is not only extrinsically unclean because he lives among tombs and in close proximity to two thousand pigs, but also intrinsically unclean because he is possessed by a legion of demons. Jesus is apparently unaffected by this. Instead, it is the man who is affected: he is restored and the impurity destroyed.

Jesus later draws attention to the fact that he has been touched by a bleeding woman (5:25–34; see also Leviticus 15:25–27). Later that same day he goes on to touch a dead child (5:38–43; see Numbers 5:2). However, the Gospel writer raises no questions about ritual defilement on the part of Jesus. Rather it is the people or the situations that are in proximity to Jesus which are transformed through their engagement with him. The dead child is raised, the bleeding woman healed and the demoniac restored to his right mind. Bleach is never affected by contact with stains; it is *always* the other way round.

CHRISTOCENTRIC HOLINESS IS MISSIONAL

If our understanding of holiness is to be distinctly Christocentric, we too must model an offensive rather than a defensive posture. Rather than viewing holiness as a fragile flower needing to be protected in an inhospitable climate of godlessness and disbelief, we might see it as light which always has the power to pierce darkness. Never underestimate what a little bit of light (or bleach!) can do.

Such an understanding of holiness is inherently missional. If we adopt a view of holiness as an offensive weapon rather than something in need of our protection, we can have a naturally open posture rather than a closed one. We don't need people to become more like us before they join the church, because we trust that the power of holiness will transform all who come into contact with Jesus, the Holy One of God. Holiness that is distinctly Christocentric is inevitably also distinctly inclusive (see above).

I'm a Methodist minister and it is my privilege to lead services of Holy Communion fairly regularly. The Methodist Church practises what is termed an open table, meaning anyone who wishes to take communion is welcome to do so, even those who are not yet in relationship with Christ. We don't do this because we're politically correct or unwilling to cause offence. Rather, we do this because we believe that taking communion is one means of experiencing God's grace and, therefore, a means of bringing us to repentance. Communion in traditional language is a 'converting ordinance'; that is, a means of bringing one to faith. Rather than keeping the sinful away from Holy Communion, we encourage the sinful to take Holy Communion because we believe that if someone encounters something of the risen Christ in the simple act of eating the bread and drinking the cup, then he or she will be transformed. We're not overly worried about someone taking the sacrament unworthily.

One of my colleagues, let's call him John, also a Methodist minister, tells a moving story of how he was converted to Christianity in a Methodist church not long after he was released from prison. He visited the church on a whim and was met at the door by an elderly woman who welcomed him and offered to sit with him. It happened to be a service of Holy Communion and when it came time for communion she whispered to him, 'This is for you, y'know. I'll come forward with you if you like.' As he went forward to the communion rail these words were said to him: 'This is the body of Christ broken for you. This is the blood of Christ, shed for you, for the forgiveness of your sins.' John says, 'When the minister said those words to me, I believed him and to my surprise came to a believing faith in Christ.'

This is in sharp contrast to a Holy Communion service I experienced one evening as a visitor to a church. One of the church members, someone I knew, came to me during a hymn to enquire whether I would like to take communion. I said yes, and he went back to his seat, wrote a note and passed it discreetly to the minister. Later, I discovered that the practice in that church was that no one who was not already a member of that fellowship was allowed to take communion unless one of the members vouched for the person, *in writing*, confirming that he or she was a worthy participant in the Lord's Supper!

OPEN AND OFFENSIVE

The different approaches to Holy Communion described above betray radically divergent perceptions of holiness. The Methodist attitude reflects an offensive position rooted in the belief that the holy is more affective than the profane. Hence, the communion table is open in order to confront everyone with the transforming holiness of Christ. The procedure in the church that I attended as a visitor reflects a naturally defensive posture rooted in the assumption that the holy somehow needs a hedge of protection around it so that the holy is not impugned and no one participates in Holy Communion unworthily. Only one of these approaches to the sacrament of Holy Communion or the Lord's Supper is distinctly Christocentric, I suggest. It's the one that reaches out, even to the sinner, as Christ did, without concern that his purity would somehow be threatened.

Understanding holiness as Christocentric – that is, Christ-centred – reflects a confidence in the transforming power of the holy and therefore exhibits something of the optimism of grace. It is rooted in the belief that the God who tells us to love our enemies also loves all he has made. It is a naturally offensive and naturally missional posture. Holy Communion, precisely because it is holy, does not need protection from the sinful and impure; instead it may be the antidote to our impurity because it is a means of mediating God's grace. Holiness is distinctly Christocentric.

When you were slaves of sin, you were free in regard to righteousness. So what advantage did you then get from the things of which you now are ashamed? The end of those things is death. But now that you have been freed from sin and enslaved to God, the advantage you get is sanctification. The end is eternal life.

(Romans 6:20–22)

Chapter eight

DISTINCTLY POSSIBLE

HOLINESS IS AN ACT OF GRACE

One of the most important things I want to communicate via this book is that holiness is possible – through God's grace. *Holiness is possible.*

Lots of us have believed a lie that holiness is not really possible this side of heaven. In the same way that we can never achieve absolute perfection, we can never really be holy. Holiness is an unattainable goal towards which we should constantly be reaching, but which we shall never grasp until we see Jesus face to face.

Of course, there is a great deal of truth in such a perspective. Indeed, I contend that this is the general perspective of Scripture. We shall not become all that God intends us to become until we see Jesus face to face (1 John 3:2). However, there is a world of difference between believing that we will not be *fully* holy until we see Jesus face to face and believing that it is not possible to be holy at all. That is not the perspective of biblical writers, for example the author of Hebrews who instructs his readers to 'Pursue peace with everyone, and the holiness without which no one will see the Lord' (Hebrews 12:14). Similarly, Paul in Romans 6:22 describes holiness as lived reality in terms of having been 'freed from sin and enslaved to God'.

As a consequence, I believe that holiness is possible. One of the reasons I believe it is possible is because we are instructed to be holy. God is not in the habit of instructing God's people to do something which is impossible for us to do. So, the fact that God commands us to be holy should fill us with hope. We can be holy.

Holiness is distinctly possible, but only by God's grace. If the ground can be holy (Exodus 3:5), mountains can be holy (Isaiah 11:9; Ezekiel 20:40) and Israel can be holy (Exodus 19:6), we too can be holy, because the same God that makes them holy also sanctifies us.

Paul's letter to the Romans, particularly chapters 6–8, wrestles with the question of sanctification; that is, the process of being made holy and set free from the power of sin.

LET'S TALK ABOUT SIN

First, a word about sin. As discussed earlier, 'sin' is not a popular word in contemporary usage. It's widely perceived as old-fashioned and, in many ways, sin is, like holiness, another 'Mufasa' word that has the capacity to send a shiver down the spine. However, when we recognize that sin is a relational word, a technical way of describing broken relationship to the Holy One and the outcomes of that brokenness, then perhaps the word makes more sense.

To describe ourselves as sinners is not primarily to make a judgment about our goodness or badness as much as it is to make a statement about our relationship to the Holy One. Similarly, forgiveness of sins is far more profound than overlooking past behaviour. It's also about restoration of right relationship to God and to one another and to creation itself.

Paul, I suggest, is also writing in a context in which most people would not naturally see themselves as sinners. However, within a Jewish-Christian context such as the church in Rome to which he was writing, the idea of sin as a way of describing broken relationship with the Holy One and its outcomes was far more common.

In Romans 6, Paul paints a compelling picture of salvation which runs far deeper than the forgiveness of sins; it's also a vision of transformed lives. In theological terms, Paul paints a picture that is not only about justification, being declared in right relationship with God, but also about sanctification, being *made* righteous and holy by God. The word 'sanctification' comes from the same Latin root word as 'saint'. One who is sanctified is a saint; that is, a holy person. It's noteworthy that Paul regularly addresses his letters, including Romans, to 'the saints'. Holy people weren't a novelty for him. They were everyday Christians.

The picture Paul paints is one of God's abundant grace: God's love, mercy, favour and blessing which cannot be earned. However, that grace requires sinful action to be left behind. In Romans 6:2, Paul asks the penetrating question: 'How can we who died to sin go on living in it?' Paul is interested in the question of how the power of sin is broken and he comes up with two striking images. First, he describes believers as dead to sin and, second, as slaves of righteousness. Dead and slaves – he really knows how to sell it!

DEAD TO SIN

What does it mean to be dead to sin? In his commentary on Romans, Durham New Testament scholar Charles Cranfield suggests four possibilities:

1 Christians have died to sin in God's sight; that is, in a forensic sense.
2 Christians have died to sin in sacramental sense; that is, in baptism.

3 Christians have died to sin in a moral sense; that is, they mortify their sins.

4 Christians die to sin only in death.[1]

Cranfield argues that Paul uses all four meanings at various points, but he suggests that in Romans 6:2 it is meanings (1) and (2) which are paramount. Another Romans scholar, Thomas Schreiner, agrees that all four are used at various points but suggests meaning (2) is closest to Paul's intent; we die to sin in our baptism.[2]

I think Schreiner is absolutely right. However, Paul is not suggesting that baptism confers the power to overcome sin. Such a view over-emphasizes baptism when Paul is more interested in that to which baptism points, the historic death and resurrection of Christ. Baptism thus functions as shorthand for conversion to, belief in, and initiation and incorporation into Christ. Using baptismal imagery, then, Paul says that Christians have died to sin. For him, this is not mere semantics or preacher's hyperbole but part of the reality of salvation.

But there's an elephant in the room. If believers have truly died to sin, why do so few Christians seem especially saintly, or 'dead to sin'? Perhaps it's just the Christians in the part of the church that I know, but they do not seem all that dead to sin to me! At least three observations need to be made here.

First, Romans 6 does not say that sin has died; rather it is the one baptized into Christ who has died. Sin is therefore still very much around, though the one who has died to sin is no longer enthralled by it. Therefore, as New Testament scholar Ben Witherington puts it, 'Sin no longer makes Christians an offer they can't refuse.'[3] Second, what we find in Romans 6, therefore, is not an assertion that sin is impossible for believers but rather an assertion that escape from sin's power is now possible. Third, there is an additional nuance to the idea of 'having died to sin' in the light of the now-and-not-yet nature of God's kingdom. Note the verb tenses used: 'if we *have died* with Christ, we believe that we *will also* live with him' (v. 8, my emphasis). What is in view then is a change of lordship, from that of sin to Christ, which of course shares its inherent now-and-not-yet tension. It is clear then that Romans 6:2–7 does not suggest that it is impossible for Christians to sin, nor even that we have achieved victory over sin. Rather, it says that we are no longer under sin's oppression because the end has broken into the present.

It is this now-and-not-yet 'eschatological tension' which enables us to make sense of what appears to be Paul's contradictory statements: we have died to sin, but we must also not allow sin to exercise dominion (v. 12). This is a tension between objective truth and personal truth.

My generation grew up praying for the end of apartheid in South Africa, and we were fortunate enough to live to see its demise.

At the London launch of his book *No Future without Forgiveness*, Archbishop Desmond Tutu argued that the reason South Africa had not descended into civil war after the end of apartheid was simply because it was the most prayed-for country in the world at that time. I grew up in Antigua, a former British colony, and I can't recall any prayers for the UK in any of the churches I attended. But we seemed to pray for South Africa nearly every Sunday.

That apartheid has died in South Africa does not mean that justice has yet been fully achieved. There is still a great deal of work to be done to deal with the legacy of apartheid. There is an ongoing tension between the historic reality that apartheid was abolished and the lived reality of continuing racial inequality. This is not too dissimilar to the tension between Paul's declaration that we have died to sin and the working out of that truth in our lives now.

ENSLAVED TO RIGHTEOUSNESS

Romans does not only speak of holiness in terms of being dead to sin; even more radically, it goes on to speak of holiness in terms of becoming slaves to righteousness. For Paul, freedom from sin is not a freedom for ourselves, but for God. It is this freedom *for God* which he describes as becoming slaves of righteousness. This enslavement is a willing one, in which we recognize that it is only through it that we experience the merits of grace. Karl Barth, one of the foremost theologians of the twentieth century, observes:

> if all that is in us does not stretch towards a sanctified life
> prepared for us and open to the righteousness of God, if we
> do not long for a life running so nigh to the righteousness of
> God that it would break through in our members, in our
> mortal body; – grace is not grace.[4]

It's not clear whether Paul is suggesting that holiness is *evidence* of becoming a slave of righteousness or that holiness *enslaves* to righteousness, but scholars have suggested that Paul has both possibilities in mind. Holiness is both the outcome and the means of enslavement to righteousness.[5]

We are perhaps more naturally familiar with the idea of being enslaved by our sinfulness or weakness. But Paul is not shy about using the imagery of enslavement to describe discipleship. His favourite way of introducing himself in his letters is as a slave of Christ. A slave does what his or her master requires and is a possession of the master, and this is the picture that Paul paints by using the same word and imagery (Romans 1:1). In the same way that we can imagine our sinfulness constraining us, Paul envisages becoming enslaved to holiness so that despite our best efforts to the contrary we end up acting in ways consistent with God's holiness. This is made much more explicit in Romans 6:22: 'But now you that have been freed from sin and enslaved to God, the advantage you get is sanctification. The end is eternal life.' Paul does not see eternal life as a *quid pro quo* for holy living in this life.

Rather salvation is a matter of grace, from start to finish. Moreover, sanctification does not happen when one obtains eternal life; rather it is understood to *lead to eternal life*, as iniquity leads to death. Sanctification is therefore rooted in this life, although it is in anticipation of the next. Holiness is distinctly possible.[6]

ROLE OF THE SPIRIT

Holiness in Romans is part of the work of the Holy Spirit. We find this explicitly expressed in the joyous beginning to Romans 8:2: 'the law of the Spirit of life . . . has set you free from the law of sin and of death.' The interesting phrase 'the spirit of holiness' occurs in Romans 1:4. Many biblical scholars gloss over this reference, seeing it merely as an unusually phrased way of alluding to the Holy Spirit. However, as New Testament scholar Tom Wright points out:

> we know from many of Paul's letters that his opening passages
> are often carefully crafted with an eye to what he wants to say
> in the rest of the letter. It seems very unlikely that he would
> place in such a prominent position an explicit statement . . .
> he regarded as at best inadequate and at worst misleading.[7]

Instead the phrase might be best understood as 'the spirit who gives holiness', an idea picked up in Romans 15:16 where Paul's Gentile converts are explicitly referred to as 'sanctified by the Holy Spirit'.[8]

DISTINCTLY POSSIBLE

Holiness in Romans, then, is very much rooted in Paul's understanding of salvation through the gift of God and in terms of death to sin and our enslavement to righteousness. Such an understanding of holiness is rooted in divine action: the gift of God, the death of Christ and the power of the Spirit. Put more simply, human holiness is an act of grace. Holiness is indeed distinctly possible, but only by the grace of God.

Therefore let us go
on towards perfection,
leaving behind the basic
teaching about Christ,
and not laying again the
foundation: repentance
from dead works and
faith towards God,
instruction about baptisms,
laying on of hands,
resurrection of the dead,
and eternal judgement.
And we will do this,
if God permits.

(Hebrews 6:1–3)

Chapter nine

DISTINCTLY HOPEFUL

HOLINESS IS A FORETASTE OF PERFECTION

The writer of the book of Hebrews encourages his readers to continue to grow in discipleship. However, the language he uses is striking: 'go on to maturity or perfection'. Notice that he doesn't say, 'You lot need to grow up.' Rather he says, 'let *us go on* towards perfection' (emphasis added). Even better, he goes on to say: '*And we will do this, if God permits.*'

At a time when many feel less than hopeful about holiness because it seems too out of reach and we seem too unremarkable to attain it – especially when the language of perfection is used – here is a refreshingly hopeful aspiration: 'we will do this, if God permits' (Hebrews 6:3). We will go on to perfection.

The word translated 'perfection' in Hebrews comes from the Greek root word *telos* which means 'end, pointing towards conclusion, consummation and fulfilment' rather than 'that which cannot be improved'. Indeed, in Hebrews, perfection points primarily towards the completion of God's plan of salvation.[1]

When the Maps app on your smartphone announces: 'You have reached your destination', it is saying you have reached your *telos*. You have completed your journey, arrived where you set off to go. *Telos* therefore carries the meaning of becoming what you were intended to be, being fully formed, or fully grown, mature. If holiness is our *telos*, a way of describing who we are meant to become in Christ, then holiness is not out of reach or reserved for the super-Christian; holiness is what mature Christianity looks like, because holiness is what God looks like.

The book of Hebrews is a helpful conversation partner for unpacking a little further this idea of holiness as perfection. It speaks of perfection, maturity, sanctifying, holiness, being holy, and a purified conscience. Clearly, there is some overlap of meaning in these terms, but a number of nuances emerge in any exploration of holiness in Hebrews.

BELIEVERS ALREADY SANCTIFIED

Perhaps one of the most striking aspects of the idea of holiness in Hebrews is that the writer takes for granted both the holiness of

God and the holiness of God's people. Hebrews repeatedly describes Christians either as already sanctified or as being sanctified in and through the definitive act of Jesus Christ in his life, death, resurrection and ascension – the people of God are holy because God makes them so. David Peterson, a renowned Hebrews scholar, observes that for the writer of Hebrews the sanctification of Christians is complete.[2]

For example, Hebrews 10:10 asserts: 'it is by God's will that *we have been sanctified* through the offering of the body of Jesus Christ once for all.' Hebrews 10:14 is similarly strident: 'by a single offering *he has perfected for all time those who are sanctified*', while Hebrews 2:11 affirms that 'the one who sanctifies and *those who are sanctified* all have one Father'.[3] The phrase 'those who are sanctified' in 2:11 and 10:14 can also be translated 'those who are being sanctified'. Given the emphasis of 10:10 it is possible that we are meant to pick up both meanings: we are both *sanctified* and *being sanctified* through the offering of Jesus Christ.

In the Old Testament, which provides the theological foundation blocks for the argument of Hebrews, it is God, the Holy One of Israel, who is primarily the one who sanctifies.[4] Here in Hebrews it is Christ who sanctifies; that is, makes holy. That Christ sanctifies is important for the writer of Hebrews for at least two reasons. First, he wants to remind us about the supremacy of Christ; second, he has a unique perspective on the high priesthood of Christ.

THE SUPREMACY OF JESUS CHRIST

Remember the Bourne films? To be honest it's probably best to forget the last two and concentrate on the original trilogy: *Bourne Identity*, *Bourne Supremacy* and *Bourne Ultimatum*. These films introduce Jason Bourne, whose capabilities are so advanced that he is a one-man army. If Jason Bourne is on your side, you will inevitably triumph. The writer of Hebrews has a not dissimilar picture of Jesus. We are introduced to God's pre-existent Son through whom the worlds were created (1:2), whom angels worship (1:6) and who is now seated at the right hand of the Father (1:3). This pre-existent Son is the exact imprint of God's very being (1:3) and, in the words of the New Testament scholar Barnabas Lindars, reaches 'fullest expression in the Jesus of history'.[5]

The humanity of Jesus also receives special emphasis in Hebrews. Jesus is made a little lower than the angels (2:9), is not ashamed to call us brothers and sisters (2:11) and is like us in every respect, yet without sin (4:15). Thus, *we have* a great high priest.

JESUS AS HIGH PRIEST

Perhaps the unique contribution of Hebrews to New Testament theology is to perceive the work and ministry of Jesus the Christ through the lens of the ministry of the Jewish high priest on the Day of Atonement. The theologian D. Stephen Long comments: 'Hebrews alone presents Jesus as the true high priest.'[6]

The author of Hebrews is doing something highly creative and theologically significant in his choice of description of Jesus as great high priest. Surprisingly, no other New Testament writers use Day of Atonement imagery to reflect on the redemptive work of Christ. In so doing, the writer of Hebrews introduces something new into New Testament perceptions. That Jesus is the one who sanctifies believers is an outworking of this idea of Jesus as our great high priest.

Hebrews 4:15 notes that we do not have a high priest who is unable to 'sympathize with our weaknesses'. Sympathy here does not indicate 'feeling sorry for' but rather 'solidarity with' – in other words, empathy. Weakness means whatever is endured because of the human condition, including temptation. This capacity to sympathize is not *despite* the greatness of our high priest but precisely *because* of his greatness. Jesus has been tested and tempted in every respect that we are, yet without committing sin.

Nonetheless, our high priest has 'passed through the heavens' (4:14). The climax of Israelite high priesthood was the responsibility of passing through the veil in the temple to enter the holy of holies, once per year on the Day of Atonement, to offer sacrifice for sins. But Jesus has passed through the heavens; he is exalted and seated at the right hand of God. While earthly high priests came face to face with the ark of the covenant, Jesus Christ is face to face with God. In the understanding of Hebrews, Jesus, therefore, does not merely *ascend*; he also *transcends* the limits of time and space.[7]

In using priesthood imagery, Hebrews redefines its understanding of priesthood in terms of self-sacrifice by pointing to the unique priesthood of Christ. Instead of offering sacrifices to God, Jesus offers himself as the single willing sacrifice. In this view of priesthood, sacrifice is no longer the offering of something external to the priest, but the free offering of oneself to God.[8] This redefinition has implications for ongoing understandings of the nature of discipleship for all who would be followers of Christ.

DISTINCTLY HOPEFUL

Holiness in Hebrews, shaped by its radical perception of the self-sacrificial nature of the high-priestly ministry of Christ, is a challenging ideal but nonetheless a distinctly hopeful one. Despite its high ideals Hebrews does not present holiness as being out of reach for mere mortals like us, because holiness is perceived from the perspective of the end. Put more elegantly, Hebrews is thoroughly *eschatological* in character – it *looks towards the end*. The book is written from the perspective that the end has already begun in the definitive act of Christ in the past, in his life, death, resurrection and ascension, which has implications for the present and will reach its fulfilment in the future. Given this end (*telos*), we can work backwards from that future to our present.

The writer of Hebrews sees reality and thus Christian discipleship through the lens of one who has already made, in himself, the perfect sacrifice for sins, and who has sanctified, in himself, his sisters and brothers. In Christ we encounter one who has gone beyond the veil into the presence of God to be a mediator of a new covenant based on better promises than those of the old covenant (Hebrews 12:24). Importantly, as the pioneer (Hebrews 2:10; 12:2), Christ goes *before* us rather than *instead of* us into the presence of God.

For the writer of Hebrews, Jesus is Nigella Lawson. Stay with me … As is the case in most televised cooking shows, Nigella shows you how to achieve perfection, whether a roast, cake or exotic dessert. The point of the exercise is not for Nigella to cook *instead* of you. Rather, she has gone *ahead* of you. She's worked out the ingredients, the optimal method, and in true *Blue Peter* style can point to the one she 'prepared earlier' as a way of showing what the outcome should be. Perhaps the best thing about TV cooks and domestic goddesses such as Nigella is that they give us hope that we mere mortals can achieve things beyond our perceived capability or even imagining.

Jesus is already seated at the right hand of the Father; he has already offered the perfect sacrifice, in himself, and in so doing has perfected for all time those who are sanctified. As the pioneer of faith, he demonstrates that holiness, something that many of us think is beyond our capability or even imagining, is not merely possible but is the norm for all who obey him.

That's why it's so important for the writer of Hebrews that the one whose self-offering definitively dealt with sin and has the power to perfect us was himself tempted just as we are. Therefore, we can come boldly to the throne of grace (Hebrews 4:16) because Jesus knows what we need. Jesus is not only high priest but also pastor and example.

Hence, Hebrews is not merely interested in Jesus' death, resurrection and ascension; it is also interested in the quality of his life. Hebrews 5:8–9 makes the interesting observation that 'although he was a Son, he learned obedience through what he suffered; and having been made perfect, he became the source of eternal salvation for all who obey him'. Put another way, the one in whom we are made perfect was himself perfected. This is not intended to allude to some imperfection in Christ but is showing that Jesus is in solidarity with humanity.

References to Jesus' flesh, loud cries, tears and death (Hebrews 5:7) testify to the fact that he is one of us, obedient even to death on a cross. It is by means of that radical obedience that Jesus is perfected. Although he is the pre-existent Son, he 'learned obedience through what he suffered', namely death. Bearing in mind that the word 'perfect' comes from the root word *telos*, the meaning of which points towards consummation and fulfilment, it is through obedience even to death that Christ is able to be the perfect high priest.

The one who lived our life and offered full obedience to the Father is the one who is now seated at the right hand of the throne of God and who not only calls us to obedience but also empowers us by his Spirit to 'run with perseverance the race that is set before us, looking to Jesus the pioneer and perfecter of our faith' (Hebrews 12:1–2). In the light of the greatness of this salvation, the writer of Hebrews is distinctly hopeful about the possibilities for human holiness.

NOW AND NOT YET

As the idea of holiness in Hebrews is eschatologically nuanced – that is, shaped by a perspective rooted in the finished work of Christ – we find that even though the sanctification of believers is assumed, they are nonetheless urged to pursue holiness, without which none shall see the Lord. Hebrews scholar Craig Koester notes this tension; the readers have already been made holy through Christ's sacrifice (9:14) but do not yet fully share in God's holiness (12:10).[9] Koester goes on to say: 'In Hebrews pursuing holiness means trusting in what Christ's death has accomplished and maintaining hope for everlasting life with God.'[10]

Perhaps it is in this way that holiness is most distinctly hopeful. To be holy is to seek by God's grace to become more deeply now what we will be most fully then, when we see the Lord. Thus, holiness is ultimately a foretaste of perfection.

I consider that the sufferings of this present time are not worth comparing with the glory about to be revealed to us. For the creation waits with eager longing for the revealing of the children of God . . .

(Romans 8:18–19)

Chapter ten

DISTINCTLY POWERFUL

HOLINESS AS TRANSFORMING POWER

I am profoundly interested in the question of holiness. I long to be holy. I'm captivated by the ideals of the beauty of holiness. I'm fully persuaded that the church universal and all creation finds fullest expression only in its true vocation of right relationship with the Holy One of Israel and it is that very relationship that enables our holiness. Mostly, however, I am inspired by holiness as God's power that results in transformation: from sinner to saint, leper to clean, darkness to light, common to sanctified, fractured and broken to whole and complete.

Throughout this book, we've viewed holiness through a number of lenses. Holiness as distinctly problematic (we so easily get it wrong), precious (important because it's important to God), divine (the core of God's being), complex (different models capture that complexity). Holiness is distinctively inclusive (a reflection of a God of justice), human (worked out in the messiness of human life), Christocentric (as modelled offensively by Jesus), possible (through the work of Jesus) and hopeful (a foretaste of the perfection of the coming kingdom).

One of the common threads through all of those perspectives on holiness is the idea of holiness as distinctly powerful, because of its transformational potential. Such transformation is only truly valuable to the church if it is also *conformation* to the image of Christ and to the mission of God.

Mission is a key biblical and theological concept, which should be understood primarily as a description of the activity of God and only secondarily as an activity of the church. The good news of the gospel, and indeed the entire narrative of the Bible, may be summarized in this: that God has a grand missional plan of reconciling all creation to himself. Such an understanding of mission leads to a number of observations.

First, this means that Christian mission needs to be set into a wider context than the church. God is profoundly interested in the church. However, over and above that, God is interested in God's kingdom, and indeed all creation.

Second, human engagement in mission is at best joining the prior activity of God. Wherever the church might engage in mission, we discover a holy God always ahead of us, seeking to draw creation back to its first vocation of loving its creator.

Third, such an understanding requires the church to be interested in more than making new Christians. Let me be absolutely clear. I believe that the church, especially in the UK, needs to be more engaged in encouraging and challenging both its members and those who are not yet members to become authentic followers of Jesus. We need a greater rather than lesser commitment to evangelism. Nonetheless, God has a broader mission than making new disciples. God is interested in the redemption of all creation (Romans 8:18). God is, therefore, deeply concerned with justice and human flourishing, and longs for creation to become all that is divinely intended.

One of the complexities of holiness is that we use the same word to describe both the *status* of being holy and the *outcomes* of being holy. We use the word 'holy' to describe a person or place in right relationship with God. We then go on to use that same word to describe both the consequences and outcomes of being in right relationship with God. Put (perhaps too) simply, holiness describes both who we are by God's grace and what we do or indeed what God is able to do in us by grace. It can therefore become difficult to keep track of whether we are talking about holiness as status or as outcomes.

An additional challenge of speaking of holiness lies in our human-centric inclinations. *All* things that belong to God are holy;

however, we Christians are very interested in what it means for human beings to be holy but perhaps less so in what it means for the very creation to be holy. Even the above paragraph, where I outlined the struggle in using the word 'holy' to describe both who *we are* and what *we do*, is an example of a human-centric approach. I might have been better placed to describe the tension in terms of *who God is* versus *what God does*. Thinking of holiness as transforming power leads us to ask: if the whole world were transformed by holiness, what might it look like?

REDEMPTION OF THE COSMOS

What we are really exploring by this question is the redemption of all creation, the cosmos. The *kosmos* in ancient Greece was a way of describing the universe, the sum of everything that exists. Paul in 2 Corinthians 5:19 uses this word to describe a vision of redemption that is more expansive than all the people in the world becoming reconciled to God, for it includes the whole of creation. Romans 8:19 similarly describes creation as waiting 'with eager longing for the revealing of the children of God'. Revelation 21:1 presents a vision of a new heaven and new earth which expresses similar hope of a renewed creation as God's ultimate plan of salvation.

What might the redemption of the cosmos have to do with holiness? If we understand holiness, first as who God is and second as being in right relationship to that holy God or under the sphere of influence of or belonging to that holy God, then the redemption of the cosmos, a world that God in Christ has fully reconciled to himself, is ultimately a vision of a holy world. This is holiness *as status*. The *outcomes* of this holiness are a new heaven and new earth. This is a world transformed by holiness.

If we cast our minds back to the account of creation in Genesis, at each stage of creation we encounter the repeated phrase 'God saw that it was good', six times for each of the six days of creation concluded by a seventh pronouncement at the end of his work: 'God saw everything that he had made, and indeed, it was very good' (Genesis 1:31). Following that pronouncement of the creation as very good we get the first biblical use of the word 'holy': 'God blessed the seventh day and hallowed it, because on it God rested from all the work that he had done in creation' (Genesis 2:3).[1]

However, this is not the way we encounter the world. That the cosmos is itself in need of redemption is a way of saying that all is not right with the world. Creation is not the way God intended it to be. This is as true of non-human as it is of human creation. Moreover, given the impact of humanity on creation, we are part of the reason why creation is not quite the way that it should be.

AN ENDURING ESCHATOLOGICAL HOPE

The redemption of the cosmos is an enduring eschatological hope. The redeemed cosmos of the coming kingdom of God is one in which justice has been established, inequities addressed, the righteous rewarded and the wicked punished, ancient enmities reconciled and hope fulfilled, and one in which the disordered, dysfunctional, diseased and decaying is reordered, restored and resurrected. Ultimately, it's a vision of a world in which tears have been wiped away and the wolf lives with the lamb. Lest we think this is an exclusively Christian or recent hope, hear these words from Isaiah: 'Then the Lord GOD will wipe away the tears from all faces, and the disgrace of his people he will take away from all the earth, for the LORD has spoken' (Isaiah 25:8). Jesus' miracles are signs of the kingdom of God, signs of a coming day when the whole cosmos will be reconciled to God in Christ and transformed by holiness. It seems to me that this kingdom vision might helpfully be portrayed in three sets of transformation: transformed humanity; transformed relationship between humanity and creation; and transformed creation.

TRANSFORMED HUMANITY

At the risk of betraying my own human-centric inclination, let's begin with humanity. In a world transformed by holiness, we shall see a transformed humanity which reflects the nature of God. This is a world in which justice is both personal and systemic. A world in which armed conflict, xenophobia, racism and sexism are curtailed not by legislation but by the transformation of humanity in holiness. That curtailment would destroy the contexts in which abuse, exploitation, human trafficking and murder find space to flourish. Imagine what the economic outcomes might be if cooperation rather than competition were the primary driver of economic output. Imagine what the implications might be if everyone paid their taxes and our elected officials always looked beyond self and party interests.

Western democracies, which were deeply shaped by Christian convictions, naturally reach towards these ideals and seek to enshrine them in our laws. However, we can never reach those ideals until all humanity is transformed so that we more fully reflect the holiness of God. Until then it is our responsibility to continue to work to see those ideals more fully embedded in our communities as signs of the coming kingdom of God.

TRANSFORMED RELATIONSHIP BETWEEN HUMANITY AND CREATION

A world transformed by holiness is one in which the relationship between humanity and creation is radically reordered. Creation could no longer be seen as primarily for human consumption. Rather all humanity would share the perspective of the psalmist:

> The earth is the LORD's and all that is in it,
>   the world, and those who live in it;
> for he has founded it on the seas,
>   and established it on the rivers.

> Who shall ascend the hill of the LORD?
>> And who shall stand in his holy place?
> Those who have clean hands and pure hearts ...
> (Psalm 24:1–4)

It's striking that the psalmist places his assertion of the divine ownership of creation together with his searching question 'Who shall stand in God's holy place?' I don't think this is a coincidence. Standing in God's holy place requires appropriate recognition of God's ownership of the earth. Remember one of our earlier models of holiness? That which is within God's sphere of influence or belonging. To declare that the earth is the Lord's is another way of describing it as holy, a sacred space.

Transformed relationship between human and non-human creation would inevitably result in deeper concern and engagement with sustaining the environment, addressing climate change, stimulating biodiversity and tackling pollution. Questions of justice that arise out of these issues would also be addressed; those who are poorest often bear the brunt of the outcomes of environmental damage. Who can stand in God's holy place? Those who have clean hands.

TRANSFORMED CREATION

The vision of a world transformed by holiness is not only one in which humanity's relationship with non-human creation is redeemed and restored but also one in which creation itself is transformed. Isaiah captures some of this in his vision of the wolf and the lamb living together. This reconciliation between predator and prey becomes a metaphor for a disordered creation being restored to order.

Does a redeemed creation no longer experience hurricanes and thunderstorms, earthquakes, floods and drought? Or do these natural disasters remain but become themselves redeemed and transformed by God's holiness? I confess that I'm at the edges of my imagination as I try to envisage what this could mean. However, I suspect the latter. Extreme weather may not disappear, any more than we disappear, but will somehow be transformed by grace into the new heaven and new earth envisaged by a number of New Testament writers.

HOLINESS AS A SIGN OF THE KINGDOM

Holiness as transforming power leads to a self-consciously utopian vision of the world, but no more so than Isaiah's vision of a banquet for all peoples and the wolf living with the lamb (Isaiah 25:6–9; 11:6–9). That utopian vision is a way of articulating our deepest hopes. Nevertheless, this is not mere utopian optimism; this is eschatology, a looking forward to the end of the age and the coming kingdom of God.

If holiness is indeed transformational, its power is not only to be experienced at the end of the age. For the kingdom of God has already begun in the life, death, resurrection and ascension of Jesus. That coming kingdom is already being experienced and continues to be spread abroad by God's Spirit outpoured at Pentecost. Though small like a mustard seed, the kingdom of God is already growing towards its final consummation.

On this basis, the transformational power of God is already at large in the world now, through the power of the Spirit. Wherever good may be found, wherever justice is experienced, wherever creation is flourishing, wherever injustice is fought, sinfulness resisted and evil confronted, wherever the environment is protected, creation celebrated, or beauty, creativity and harmony find space, there we see glimpses of the kingdom of God. Wherever the presence of God may be experienced, there too we may have a foretaste of his kingdom and of the transforming power of his holiness.

When we stretch out our hands and hearts, and expend our energies and resources, to do justice, love mercy and walk humbly with God (Micah 6:8), we seek ever more to witness to the transforming power of holiness in our world and in creation, and to experience that same transformation in our lives and communities.

Holiness is distinctly powerful, for it is nothing less than the power of the Holy One of Israel. My prayer is that we truly experience that holy transforming power of God in our communities, churches and lives. May this be your prayer as well. Amen.

Notes

1 DISTINCTLY PROBLEMATIC

1 From a sermon preached by Dr Ruth Etchells on Tuesday,
8 February 2011, at St John's College, Durham University.

2 DISTINCTLY PRECIOUS

1 R. W. L. Moberly, '"Holy, Holy, Holy": Isaiah's Vision of God',
in *Holiness Past and Present*, ed. S. C. Barton (London: T&T Clark,
2003), p. 127. YHWH is a Hebrew word which is the Israelite
covenant name for God. This word would traditionally not be
spoken aloud as it was too holy to be uttered. Hence, we are not
exactly sure how it would have been pronounced. When reading
Scripture aloud the phrase 'the LORD' would have been substituted
and in many English Bibles that phrase is used to translate this
word.

2 John Hartley, *Leviticus* (Dallas: Word, 1992), p. lvi.

3 Hartley, *Leviticus*, p. 312.

3 DISTINCTLY DIVINE

1 R. W. L. Moberly, ' "Holy, Holy, Holy": Isaiah's Vision of God',
   in *Holiness Past and Present*, ed. S. C. Barton (London: T&T Clark,
   2003), p. 127.

2 Jacob Milgrom, *Leviticus 17–22* (New York: Doubleday, 2000),
   pp. 1711–1712.

3 A Nazirite was a person dedicated to God for his whole life from
   birth. John the Baptist was most likely dedicated as a Nazirite.

4 See Milgrom, *Leviticus 17–22*, pp. 1629ff., for similar views.

4 DISTINCTLY COMPLEX

1 Jacob Milgrom, *Leviticus 17–22* (New York: Doubleday, 2000),
   p. 1397. Hartley is also of a similar view in John Hartley, *Leviticus*
   (Dallas: Word, 1992).

2 See Philip Jenson, 'Holiness in the Priestly Writings of the Old
   Testament', in *Holiness Past and Present*, ed. S. C. Barton (London:
   T&T Clark, 2003), pp. 98ff. For similar views, see also Jacob
   Milgrom, 'The Changing Concept of Holiness in the Pentateuchal
   Codes with Emphasis on Leviticus 19', in *Reading Leviticus:
   A Conversation with Mary Douglas*, ed. John F. A. Sawyer (Sheffield:
   Sheffield Academic Press, 1996), pp. 65–75.

3 Mary Douglas, *Purity and Danger* (London: Routledge, 1966), p. 57.

4 Gordon Thomas, 'A Holy God among a Holy People in a Holy Place:
   The Enduring Eschatological Hope', in *The Reader Must Understand*,
   eds. K. E. Brower and M. W. Elliott (Leicester: IVP, 1997), p. 57.

5 John Hartley, *Leviticus* (Dallas: Word, 1992), p. lvii. See also Mary Douglas, 'Sacred Contagion', in *Reading Leviticus*, ed. Sawyer, pp. 86ff., for more on the idea of sacred contagion.

6 From 'Nothing but the Blood' by Robert Lowry (1826–99).

7 From 'Blessed Be the Fountain' by Eden Reeder Latta (1839–1915).

8 From 'A Balm in Gilead', anonymous.

9 From 'Amazing Grace' by John Newton (1725–1807).

10 <https://acton.org/pub/religion-liberty/volume-4-number-2/ economics-sin-taxes>.

11 Philip Peter Jenson, *Graded Holiness* (Sheffield: JSOT Press, 1992), p. 48.

12 Christopher J. H. Wright, *Living as the People of God* (Leicester: IVP, 1983), pp. 21–22.

5 DISTINCTLY INCLUSIVE

1 Myrto Theocharous, 'Becoming a Refuge: Sex Trafficking and the People of God', *Journal of the Evangelical Theological Society*, vol. 59, no. 2 (June 2016), p. 313.

2 For more on this, see Myrto Theocharous's helpful article.

3 Christopher J. H. Wright, *Living as the People of God* (Leicester: IVP, 1983), p. 146.

4 For more, see S. H. Widyapranawa, *The Lord Is Saviour: Faith in National Crisis* (Edinburgh: Handsel Press, 1990), p. 31.

5 So argues John G. Gammie, *Holiness in Israel* (Minneapolis: Fortress Press, 1989), p. 195.

6 Gammie, *Holiness in Israel*, pp. 83ff.

7 It must be admitted that a similar word is used in Isaiah 33:8 where it is typically translated as 'one who passes along' rather than 'one who passes by'.

8 Bible translators have to make this kind of choice every now and then. When words can be translated in more than one way, they put one translation in the text and another in the footnote.

9 See Walter Harrelson, 'Isaiah 35 in Recent Research and Translation', in *Language, Theology, and the Bible*, ed. S. E. Balentine and J. Barton (Oxford: Clarendon Press, 1994), pp. 249ff.

10 Harrelson, 'Isaiah 35 in Recent Research and Translation', pp. 249–250.

6 DISTINCTLY HUMAN

1 It is well attested that the satan (*ha-satan*) here is not to be identified with the devil, but rather the accuser or prosecutor among the gathering of the sons of God (1:6–12; 2:1–7).

2 For example, R. W. L. Moberly, 'Solomon and Job: Divine Wisdom in Human Life', in *Where Shall Wisdom Be Found?* ed. Stephen C. Barton (Edinburgh: T&T Clark, 1999), pp. 9–10. For a similar view, see R. P. Scheindlin, *The Book of Job* (London: W. W. Norton, 1998), pp. 11–12.

3 Craig L. Blomberg, *Contagious Holiness* (Leicester: IVP, 2005), p. 49.

4 That Job offers his own sacrifices (1:5) suggests that the story is set in a very early period and casts Job as a neo-patriarchal figure, a bit like Abraham. I acknowledge, therefore, that ideas of exclusion from

the sacrificial cult might be anachronistic because it would not yet have been created. However, later Israelite readers would have hardly failed to notice that Job would have been considered *by them* to be leprous.

5 Admittedly, the fact that Job's comforters sit with him for seven days and nights (2:13), followed by lengthy disputations about Job's innocence or guilt, undermines any suggestions that Job was completely cut off from society.

6 Gerald Wilson wryly observes that it is surely significant that the comforters are referred to as friends of Eliphaz and not of Job. See Gerald H. Wilson, *Job* (Milton Keynes: Paternoster, 2007), p. 471.

7 See D. J. A. Clines, *Job 1–20* (Dallas: Word, 1989), p. xxxviii, for more on this idea.

8 Carl G. Jung, *Answer to Job* (London: Routledge, 1987), p. 20.

9 Jung, *Answer to Job*, p. 22.

10 For more on this, see David J. A. Clines, *Job 21–37* (Nashville: Thomas Nelson, 2006).

7 DISTINCTLY CHRISTOCENTRIC

1 See Martin Hengel, *Judaism and Hellenism* (London: SCM, 1974), p. 176.

2 See Marcus J. Borg, *Conflict, Holiness and Politics in the Teaching of Jesus* (New York: Edwin Mellen, 1984), pp. 58ff.

3 Borg, *Conflict, Holiness and Politics*, pp. 74ff.

4 For more, see <https:www.youtube.com/watch?v=fGoWLWS4-kU>.

5 See Borg, *Conflict, Holiness and Politics*, pp. 74ff., for more on this.

6 James D. G. Dunn, 'Jesus and Holiness: The Challenge of Purity', in *Holiness Past and Present*, ed. Stephen C. Barton (London: T&T Clark, 2003), p. 172.

7 See Dunn, 'Jesus and Holiness', pp. 171ff., for more on this view.

8 Dunn, 'Jesus and Holiness', p. 192.

9 For more on this, see Klaus Berger, 'Jesus als Pharisäer und frühe Christen als Pharisäer', *Novum Testamentum*, vol. 303 (1988), pp. 231–262 (240ff.).

8 DISTINCTLY POSSIBLE

1 See C. E. B. Cranfield, *The Epistle to the Romans* (Edinburgh: T&T Clark, 1975), pp. 299ff. Schreiner also has a similar view; see Thomas R. Schreiner, *Romans* (Grand Rapids: Baker, 1998), p. 305.

2 Schreiner, *Romans*, p. 305.

3 Ben Witherington III, *Paul's Letter to the Romans* (Grand Rapids: Eerdmans, 2004), p. 156.

4 Karl Barth, *The Epistle to the Romans*, trans. Edwin C. Hoskyns (London: Oxford University Press, 1933), p. 223.

5 Schreiner, *Romans*, p. 341.

6 Witherington, *Paul's Letter to the Romans*, p. 174.

7 N. T. Wright, *Paul: Fresh Perspectives* (London: SPCK, 2005), p. 44.

8 See Gordon D. Fee, *God's Empowering Presence: The Holy Spirit in the Letters of Paul* (Peabody: Hendrickson, 1994), p. 483.

9 DISTINCTLY HOPEFUL

1 For more on this, see Barnabas Lindars SSF, *The Theology of the Letter to the Hebrews* (Cambridge: Cambridge University Press, 1991), p. 44.

2 David Peterson, *Possessed by God* (Leicester: Apollos, 1995), p. 34.

3 All emphasis in the above Scripture quotations is mine.

4 It must be acknowledged, however, that there are many texts urging Israel and Israelites to *sanctify themselves*, for example Leviticus 11:44; Joshua 3:5; 1 Samuel 16:5.

5 Lindars, *Theology of the Letter to the Hebrews*, p. 34.

6 D. Stephen Long, *Hebrews* (Louisville: Westminster John Knox, 2011), p. 123.

7 So argues P. E. Hughes, *Hebrews* (Grand Rapids: Eerdmans, 1977), p. 170. See also William L. Lane, *Hebrews 1–8*, Word Biblical Commentary (Grand Rapids: Zondervan, 2015).

8 See Frank J. Matera, 'The Theology of The Epistle to the Hebrews', in *Reading the Epistle to the Hebrews: A Resource for Students*, ed. Eric F. Mason and Kevin B. McCruden (Atlanta: Society of Biblical Literature, 2011), pp. 206–207.

9 Craig R. Koester, *Hebrews* (New York: Doubleday, 2001), p. 539.

10 Koester, *Hebrews*, p. 541.

10 DISTINCTLY POWERFUL

1 I'm grateful to my doctoral student, the Revd Philip Turner, for pointing this out in his thesis on holiness.

Because when it comes to God, less isn't MORE>

MORE> books in the series

MORE> *Direction*
ISBN: 978 1 78359 710 9

MORE> *Distinct*
ISBN: 978 1 78359 708 6

Coming soon

MORE> *Real*
ISBN: 978 1 78359 768 0

MORE> *Truth*
ISBN: 978 1 78359 766 6

For **MORE>** information: ivpbooks.com/more